GRAVE TALES
FROM WALES 2

More 'Stories in Welsh Stone'

By

Geoff Brookes

Published by

Llyfrau Cambria Books, Wales, United Kingdom.

Cambria Books is a division of

Cambria Publishing Ltd.

Discover our other books at: www.cambriabooks.co.uk

Before the winter fire, I will still be dreaming.
I have no thought of time.
For who knows where the time goes?
Who knows where the time goes?

Sandy Denny

All photographs were taken by the author, Geoff Brookes, apart from the photograph of the grave of Alice Douglas-Pennant on page 46 which was taken by Will Greenwood and I am grateful for his permission to use it.

For more books by Geoff Brookes, please visit his website at

https://www.geoffbrookes.co.uk

Cover image

The Cholera Cemetery, Cefn Golau, Tredegar

CONTENTS

Introduction

This book follows the same pattern as Volume One of Grave Tales of Wales.

This time there are 35 graves from across Wales and each one opens a unique window into our history. Those graves, the physical representations of a life, connect us instantly to the past in a way nothing else can.

All of these stories appeared in one form or another in Welsh Country Magazine during the fifteen years I was writing for them. Once again, I would like to offer my sincere thanks to Ian and Kath and their team at the magazine, for the loyal encouragement I received throughout that time. I loved writing for them and discovering these different aspects of Welsh history that would otherwise have remained unknown to me. I appreciate their generosity in permitting me to present these pieces in this way.

In Volume Two, I have also included stories from our military history. As you will be aware, I do not share the talent of the poet Wilfred Owen but, like him, I have never had any desire to repeat the old lie about how glorious war is. I hope I have been able to show the people behind the medals, to show how, in so many cases, their wartime experiences became a burden they carried with them for the rest of their lives.

I have also included a small number of memorials where graves no longer exist or are inaccessible, but where is a story that should be told. We have also travelled outside Wales to track down some of those who are buried elsewhere, but still have a story that needs to be preserved. The terrible story of William Jones is justification enough for such journeys, in my opinion.

At the very end of the book, I have also included a bonus piece, the Murder Stone of Cadoxton, which I have written about before. When I saw it for the first time I was astonished; I still am. Quite simply, it is the reason why I started to write about local history. The book in which I first examined the story behind the stone (*Stories in Welsh Stone*) is now, sadly, out of print, but so many people have asked me about the gravestone, that I thought it was appropriate to repeat the story here for new readers.

You can visit any of these places, and I hope the directions I have included are sufficient to help you find them. I am completely convinced that if you do visit and take an opportunity to place your hand on the grave or the memorial, it will not only deepen your understanding, but also remind you of your own place in history. It might sound fanciful, but I do not doubt it.

Neither do I doubt that there are still remarkable stories waiting to be unearthed in every part of Wales. We merely need to find them.

Abbey Cwm Hir, Powys
Llywelyn, Ein Llew Olaf, 1282

Tricked, Trapped, Eliminated

When you seek out Llywelyn's grave, the search takes you deep into the heart of Wales, the country of which he was prince. It is a journey that also takes you deep into the past, to an unfamiliar and unknown world. A world of warfare, bloodshed, torture and treachery. A world where Llywelyn was the first - and last – native prince to be recognised by the English crown, a man still mourned almost eight hundred years later.

Where the body of Llywelyn may have been buried

Abbey Cwm Hir, the abbey in the Long Valley, is a remarkably beautiful place. On the A483, north of Llandrindod Wells, you will find a narrow road signposted Abbey Cwm Hir. This quiet road follows the Clywedog Brook and after 4 miles of twists and turns you will find it. The abbey is now a scenic ruin, a skeleton, incomplete walls, broken pillars. And where the High Altar may have been, there is now a memorial slab, marking, perhaps, the grave of Llywelyn ap Gruffydd. The last true Prince of Wales. This is where tradition says his body was put to rest.

But not his head. Oh no. They hacked that off and displayed it on a stick in London to great celebration, proof of the death of a feared enemy.

These were turbulent times. It required strength, determination and ruthlessness to maintain the fragile alliances that bound the different Welsh factions together. If you were a ruler, you couldn't even trust the rest of your family. The motivation of these tribal leaders was not the noble ambition of a unified and independent Wales. Self-interest and self-preservation came first. Maintaining unity was a full-time job, and this may go some way to explaining the background to Llywelyn's death. He had confronted the English since his succession as ruler of Gwynedd in 1255. He was a skilled military leader and a shrewd politician. In 1267 he had been recognised by the treaty of Montgomery as Prince of Wales by Henry III. This was a significant moment and the high point of his career. Such recognition had never happened before and would never happen again.

Things changed with the accession of Edward I. Failed plotters against Llywelyn were soon given asylum at the English court.

Edward declared war on Llywelyn in 1277 and outmanoeuvred him, forcing harsh terms upon him at the end of a short campaign. These terms created increasing resentment against English rule. A rebellion sparked into life when Llywelyn's brother Dafydd attacked Hawarden Castle, near Chester, in 1282.

Initially the Welsh had great success.

They defeated the English forces comprehensively at the battle of Moel y Don near Bangor on 6 November 1282. Perhaps they could indeed drive the English out of north Wales once and for all.

On the back of this success, Llywelyn seems to have decided to move south, leaving his brother in control in the north. Quite what it was that drew him south is not clear. Perhaps he needed to establish new alliances, perhaps he had received messages. Whatever it was, this march led to his death and destroyed his army.

We know that Llywelyn died in the late afternoon of Friday 11 December 1282 and the precise details are unclear. However, it is possible to piece together a coherent story, though there is much, of course, that will always remain speculative.

Where tradition says that he died

The key figures in his death appear to be Roger Mortimer and his son Edmund, who were leading the English forces in the area. Many now believe that they had created an elaborate plot to eliminate him and by so doing paralysed the Welsh insurrection. If this was their plan, then it worked perfectly.

Llywelyn arrived at Abbey Cwm Hir with a large force on 10 December and was well received by the locals, though whether their support was genuine is unclear. It could have been part of a planned deception, to draw him deeper into a trap.

The next morning he went towards Builth, leaving behind the main body of his troops. There was, it is said, a question mark over the loyalty of troops from Brecon to the English cause, and perhaps he therefore hoped that he could recruit them to his side. He must have received some indication that they might be ready to do so.

Was this, as many now believe, the final piece in an elaborate plot?

His small party was ambushed somewhere near the river Irfon at dusk on Friday 11 December 1282; traditionally believed to be at Cilmeri. All of his party were killed in a brief engagement. In such a moment history changed forever.

Evidence from letters of the Archbishop of Canterbury certainly suggests that he had been tricked, tracked and eliminated. All of Llywelyn's party were killed, even a priest. A witness silenced perhaps.

Llywelyn's head was hacked off and taken to King Edward, who had it displayed in triumph on a pole on the Tower of London for all to see. An enemy vanquished.

The rest of Llywelyn's body was taken back to Abbey Cwm Hir and buried under the high altar. Today the clear outlines of this modern tribute stand in sharp contrast to the ruins that surround it.

When the prince's head was removed, so was the head of the Welsh forces. Fortified by their success in this ambush, the English-led forces attacked the leaderless Welsh early the next morning and slaughtered them. Contemporary sources report over three thousand dead and not one English casualty, but how accurate this is we will never know. In a letter Roger Mortimer said *'Llywelyn is dead, his army defeated and all the flower of his army dead.'*

Perhaps the story of a plot and a conspiracy merely reflects the paranoia of our own troubled time. And certainly there are other stories, other myths. Believe what you will. In the end it might be better to believe the myths, than to accept that the Prince of Wales was betrayed by a Welshman.

The implications of his death were considerable.

Wales could no longer regard itself as a country separate from England. But the country needed a prince and Edward, it is said, promised the Welsh that he would give them such a prince, one who had no a stain upon his honour, one who was born in Wales and one who could speak no English.

So it was that Eleanor, Edward's queen, gave birth to a son in Caernarvon Castle. Perfect in every detail and neatly fulfilling all the criteria. He was formally declared to be Prince of Wales. It became the custom that the title was not inherited but conferred through investiture. The honour of becoming the recognised leader of the Welsh people was now a gift of the English king. It mattered little whether or not the recipient was acceptable.

The insurrection staggered on without Llewelyn for another six months in the north under the leadership of his brother Dafydd, who declared himself the new Prince of Wales. It ended in June 1283 when he was handed over to the English by *'men of his own tongue.'* The poor man was taken to Shrewsbury where he had the very dubious honour of becoming the first man to face death by being hanged, drawn and quartered. His head was sent to join that of his brother, still staring sightlessly out at London.

By the spring at Cilmeri

Every year on the anniversary of the death of 'Our prince Llywelyn,' patriots meet to remember him in a ceremony at the memorial in Cilmeri and gather around a simple stone on a mound, a piece of granite from Caernarfon where he was born, to mourn this turning point in Welsh history. The dream of an independent Wales may well have died with him on that winter's afternoon, all those years ago.

In the far corner of the site, you will find a short but steep flight of steps that leads down to the well where they might have washed his severed head before packing it away to take to the king. Lift the wooden lid and look. There always a few coins at the bottom of the well, appeasing the ancient gods who turned against the Prince.

Even if you have the place to yourself, you will be aware that others have been here before you; there are always flowers here, for Llywelyn is still remembered.

The first and last Prince of Wales.

Aberystwyth, Ceredigion
James Williams 1857

Shot in the rigging

The gravestone is ignored these days. It might have been an event once important enough to be mentioned in Parliament, but it is now long forgotten.

The stone is one of the many that line the Pay and Display car park at the end of King Street in Aberystwyth. It was moved and placed here some time ago. It is next to the church of St Michael which lies on the edge of the town, up against the sea.

The castle grounds, neat and picturesque, protect the church from the sea, though the church was not always able to protect its congregation from its dangers. There are many graves that remember death at sea – sailors lost overboard, for example. You will find such graves in all of our seaports in Wales. Men who went out to sea and never returned to their families.

When we went there to visit James Williams, generations of families were stretched out on the grass, enjoying the unexpected sun. They still had to shelter from the traditional wind off the Irish Sea that always seems to throw itself at Aberystwyth, but children played on the grass, alongside these re-sited gravestones, their histories and their stories less important now than their role as a border.

You will find an arch way in the south corner where there is a lovely inscription, which begins with the arresting words,

Stop Traveller, stop and read. This stone was erected by those who fully appreciated the integrity and fidelity of David Lewis, alias The Old Commander.

David Lewis died in 1850 at the age of 66. He had fought on the *Conqueror* under Nelson at Trafalgar and for 13 years he had been the respected Deputy Harbourmaster. He had had an opportunity to build a longer life of achievement than James Williams, the young man whose grave we had come to find.

Down by the arch, you will find the Williams boys. Squeeze past the bumpers of the cars and you will see them. Their stone has slipped down to cover those beneath it, but it remains thankfully undamaged and in excellent condition. There were three brothers. Their father James was a mercer and he and Mary had the dreadful duty of burying their three sons. John, William and James. How difficult that must have been.

The parental grief that it describes is hard to imagine. William died in July 1841 and John, their second son, who died in 1825, was only 7 weeks old. It was the death of their surviving brother, James, that had drawn us to this functional, ordinary car park.

His fate? To spend eternity in a car park.

10

At the time of his curious death at the age of 21, he was serving in the merchant navy on the schooner *John and Edward*. Just another boy from Aberystwyth working at sea; just another boy from Aberystwyth who died at sea.

His ship had left Bordeaux, heading north for Liverpool, on the 24 May 1857. A contrary wind forced them to shelter in Quiberon Bay in Brittany, in the harbour of Sarzeau on the northeast coast of Belle Isle. Since they had been driven in by the weather, the necessary signals were not ready to be hoisted and they anchored close to the stern of a French man-of-war, the *Maratch*.

The French hailed the *John and Edward* but the captain, James Evans, could not make himself understood. His language skills had clearly not been polished during convivial shore time in Bordeaux. All he could do shout was *'Liverpool!'* loudly which, in truth, did not convey the nuanced meaning required in these circumstances. This was not good enough and, in an attempt, perhaps, to prompt inadequately embedded language skills, the French captain ordered a musket to fire a shot – a blank as it turned out - to persuade the British ship to fly its flag. They were keen to know who they were.

Evans, of course, knew what his responsibilities entailed and when his wife quickly produced a flag, he ordered a member of the crew to wave it frantically. It did not have the necessary impact and a second blank shot was fired. This perhaps reflected impatience, rather than a belief that the *John and Edward* represented any sort of threat. James Williams was sent scrambling into the rigging with the flag when there was a third shot - a live one this time - that hit him as he worked to haul up the ensign. He fell to the deck. Mrs Evans later said in a letter... *'He did not sigh or groan'*.

Captain Evans immediately launched a boat and went to the *Maratch* to tell them what had happened. They in their turn, sent their doctor across, but it was too late. James was dead and was buried in Belle Isle.

Mr Lewis Dillwyn, MP for Swansea, outlined these unnecessary events in Parliament and his comments were duly recorded in Hansard. It was the Prime Minister, Viscount Palmerston, who replied to the issues he raised. He confirmed that the first two shots were blank musket rounds. He acknowledged that the *John and Edward* was at fault, for '*no ship ought to enter the harbour of a foreign country without colours to distinguish her nationality*,' but there was certainly no justification in ordering a live round to be fired at the ship.

The French officer from the *Maratch* told an enquiry that he ordered the shot to be fired deliberately high but '*the ball glanced and unfortunately the shot took effect.*'

Even before the British government could complain, the French had called in the British Ambassador in Paris and Count Walewski offered a full apology of '*the most satisfactory and handsome kind*,' according to Palmerston. Orders had already been given to '*dismiss from the French service the officer who had given orders to fire the fatal musket shot*,' which provoked cries of '*hear, hear*,' in the House. Palmerston's reassurances that the French government wanted to '*mitigate the affliction of the family of the unfortunate seaman*' led to cheers. How easily the House was moved to emotion, even in those days. In fact, Palmerston was impressed by the way the whole incident had been handled, certainly in ways which would not impact adversely upon the Williams family back in Aberystwyth. '*Nothing can be more honourable and proper than the manner of their proceeding towards the English Government on the subject*,' he said. International relations restored; a difficulty managed by careful diplomacy. How very noble and supportive. But cold comfort to a family that had now lost its third son.

The Williams family were supported by their MP Captain Pryce, and with his assistance, Sir Anthony Perrier, Her Majesty's Consul in Brest, arranged for James to be sent home. He arrived in Aberystwyth with full honours on 1 August 1857 on the *Bonne Emilie* and was reburied in his home town.

What satisfaction could be rendered has been given by the French Government, and the wishes of the friends of the deceased have been complied with, in having his remains brought here, to be deposited amongst those of his relatives.

The perfidious French. The press did not miss the opportunity to emphasise the patriotic details – a young boy in the rigging, tangled up in the Union Jack and killed by a musket shot that had gone through both James and the precious flag. However you want to present it, the fact remained that he was dead. But a major diplomatic incident was avoided through carefully choreographed compassion. The right things were said, and the world moved on. But a family was left to grieve.

James Williams was an ordinary boy from Aberystwyth who became an unexpected issue for the Prime Minister and then a family tragedy was carefully managed by the Civil Service, so well in fact, that now his gravestone is a forgotten part of the boundary of a Pay and Display car park above the sea in Aberystwyth.

And what of his ship? The *John and Edward?* That was lost too, in a severe storm off Holyhead in October 1858.

Amlwch, Anglesey.
William Williams VC, 1965

Love for Sail

We went to Amlwch to find a man called William Williams. Not difficult perhaps, since there have been lots of men in Wales called William Williams. This one, though, won a Victoria Cross in 1917. In fact, there have been two Welshmen with this name who received the ultimate recognition of their bravery. The other came from Monmouthshire and died in action at Gallipoli. A courageous man certainly, but the grave I went to see represents an astonishing story from Amlwch's past and a remarkable part of our history.

A modest grave for a modest man

William's whole life was based around the sea. His father had been a fisherman – and latterly the town crier – and he enlisted in the Royal Naval Reserve as a seaman. But his life was unexpectedly defined by German submarines, which carried out systematic attacks on merchant shipping, in an attempt to destroy the food chain linking Britain and America. Tons of meat and grain sank to the bottom of the Atlantic, lost forever. These secret killers came with no warning. There were no systems available to detect them. The first anyone knew was when a torpedo stuck them. Once the U boat had disabled a vessel, they had sufficient gun power when they surfaced to destroy a ship long before the Royal Navy could arrive to affect a rescue.

The solution was Q ships. The government requisitioned ships from their owners and converted them into armed vessels. They looked innocent enough, but they had heavy guns concealed behind screens. They were crewed by volunteers like Williams, who took remarkable risks. For the deception to work, the crew had to ensure that they were successfully attacked by patrolling U boats. They were instructed that, if necessary, they had to slow down to ensure that German torpedoes hit them. Then the crew would abandon the wounded ship. This was the 'panic party,' who added verisimilitude by carrying stuffed parrots in cages, or sometimes by dressing as women. The submarine would surface to destroy the ship and then a second crew left behind would reveal themselves and attack. They had to act quickly and decisively, or the U boat would submerge and finish the job with torpedoes.

Of course, the strategy was fraught with dangers. It was illogical, incredibly dangerous and rather mad. At any point, the Q ship could have been destroyed by a suspicious submarine that refused to consider taking any risks at all. But the loss of a ship – and its crew - was felt to be a price worth paying if it could neutralise just one silent killer. As a result, Q ships stalked the sea like deadly street walkers.

Williams' first action was in January 1917 on board *HMS Farnborough*, which sank the U 83 off the coast of Ireland. They were hit by a torpedo and began to sink but waited and waited until the submarine surfaced and came close enough for them to attack it decisively. For his role in this action as part of the gun crew, he received the Distinguished Service Medal. You might think that such a close encounter with mortality would have been sufficient, but Williams now had a taste for it. He was transferred to a Cardiff-based ship, initially called the *Vittoria*, then *HMS Snail* but it was as *HMS Pargust* that she sailed into triumph, in her dangerous and deadly seduction of U boats.

In June 1917 she successfully enticed a submarine into a brief but productive relationship. *HMS Pargust* was suddenly hit by a torpedo which ripped a hole in the hull and killed Stoker Radford. The explosion also dislodged the dummy cabin, behind which the starboard gun was hidden. If the structure had fallen, it would have exposed the ship's true purpose, and so the deception needed to be maintained at all costs. And this is the vital part that William Williams played.

The 'Panic party' abandoned ship, whilst U 29 raised its periscope and warily circled the *Pargust,* alive to the possibility of trickery. Eventually, 30 minutes after the initial attack, it was sufficiently reassured. It surfaced and moved slowly round towards the stern of the *Pargust*. All this time Commander Campbell held his nerve, waiting for the best possible moment – which came when the submarine was less than 50 yards away. They opened fire with devastating results. The first shot went right through the conning tower. There were a further 37 shots fired. At one point, the crew appeared to surrender and firing ceased. But when the submarine then tried to escape, like an unfaithful lover, the attack resumed and ten minutes after surfacing there was an explosion and the U boat sank. Only two men survived. Twenty-three men, including the captain, were killed. A U boat which had previously sunk seventeen ships and had been laying mines off the coast of Ireland, had been neutralised. The sea was a little safer.

The *Pargust*, despite serious damage, did not sink and was towed slowly back to Plymouth, ready to fight another day, ready to establish new relationships. As a consequence, the ship as a unit was nominated for a VC under the 'ballot system.' This permitted the crew to vote for one officer and one seaman to receive the medal on behalf of everyone. One went to Lieutenant Ronald Stuart and the other was awarded to William Williams. The latter was no surprise at all, since the success of the whole deception rested, literally, upon his shoulders. In the initial torpedo attack, the explosion seriously loosened the whole artifice. The screens shielding the guns had started to fall and it was Williams who had supported the whole structure, thus maintaining the deception. In doing this, he ensured that the U boat came within range, whilst sustaining a serious injury to his back which affected him for the rest of his life. But without his strength and his obduracy, the guns would not have remained hidden and the submarine would not have been sunk – and his colleagues would not have survived. Perhaps it was an unexpected way to receive the Victoria Cross, but the fact that he was nominated by his comrades makes the award all the more worthy and significant.

Of course, the crew of the *Pargust* were determined to continue their seduction of submarines. Their deception was addictive. Williams and colleagues volunteered to join Commander Campbell on the *Dunraven*, another Cardiff collier. It was disguised as the *Boverton* and sailed flirtatiously into the Bay of Biscay to charm torpedoes from the cold sea. This time though they were only partly successful. Yes, they did attract the attentions of a submarine. Yes, they were hit by a torpedo. But the German captain, wary and unconvinced, reluctant to establish any sort of relationship, kept his distance and sailed away once the *Boverton* had sunk. You can't win them all – and nothing could detract from the bravery and the heroism of the *Pargust*.

Naturally, Amlwch was immensely proud of Williams. There was public acclamation and presentations. But the injuries he sustained on the Pargust meant that he was unable to continue his service. He never went back to sea, though he ended his service as the most highly decorated seaman in the Royal Navy. He also received the Medaille Militaire from France – a medal rarely awarded to a foreign national.

Williams was a modest man and anonymity was surely not impossible to find for a man in Wales called William Williams. But in Holyhead and Amlwch there was only one - the one known as *'Will VC.'* Significant recognition. And he was not chosen by distant officers behind a desk, reading reports, but by his comrades, by the men who saw him in action, who knew their lives had been saved because of what he did. He often said, with typical modesty, that he had won the VC *'in a raffle'* - but it must have meant a great deal to have such respect from his comrades. Amlwch loved him too. In June after he had received the Distinguished Service Medal, *'the town was gaily decorated with banners and bunting'* and there was a procession led by the *'Menai Bridge Bugle Band.'* It was all part of what the North Wales Chronicle described as *'Honour for Amlwch Hero.'* He received the VC in July 1917, though the nature of his heroism was never detailed, to preserve the secrecy of the Q ship operation. It was called the 'mystery VC.'

He died in 1965 and the grave he shares in Amlwch Cemetery with his second wife is easy to find. Go through the gates and it is in section on the right-hand side. Square and neat. Well kept. Precise. And it shelters both a brave man and a remarkable story.

Bala, Gwynedd

Betsi Cadwaladr
Buried in Abney Park Cemetery, London

That Wild Woman from the Welsh Hills

What we see here is a memorial to her that was erected in her honour in Abney Park Cemetery in London. She was originally buried in a shared pauper's grave, the location of which has been lost in the tangled neglect and the Victorian splendour.

Finally remembered

19

In the one surviving picture that we have of Betsi she is sitting, dressed in Welsh flannel with shawl and bonnet, looking rather stern. She might be a mamgu from a low stone cottage in the mountains but in fact, she travelled the world and became one of the first heroines in nursing history.

Elizabeth Cadwaladr was born in May 1789 on a farm called Pen Rhiw, in the hills above Bala. She was one of 16 children and a life of domestic duty and hard physical labour lay ahead of her. However, the death of her mother when she was only five affected her profoundly. She became a rebellious child and to escape the strict rules of her father Dafydd, a Methodist preacher, she went to live with their landlord when she was nine. She learnt all the domestic skills whilst she was there and, most importantly of all, she learnt English. It was this that was to be her passport out of the hills.

At the age of 14 Betsi ran away to see the world. She decided to start in Chester where she had an aunt. When she arrived the aunt gave her the money for the coach back to Bala but instead, she used it to take a boat to Liverpool.

Here she went into domestic service and changed her name. Cadwaladr was far too difficult for the English to pronounce, so she adopted the name of Davis. She worked variously as a maid, a housekeeper and a nurse. With other employers she travelled throughout Europe. In 1815 she found herself in Brussels at the time of the Battle of Waterloo and later told of how she helped to tend the wounded lying on the field in the days following the battle. Back in Liverpool the following year, she became secretly engaged to Captain Thomas Harris but, two days before the wedding, he drowned when his ship, *The Perseverance*, was wrecked.

Her father went to Liverpool to bring her home, but instead she ran off to London. In 1820 she became nanny to a sea captain's family and spent the greatest part of her life sailing the world. Hers was a life full of adventure and incident. At one point she married an engineer in the East Indies, though how much of an adventure that was, I can't say.

On her return to London however, she somehow lost her savings and had no means of otherwise supporting herself. She began nursing in Guy's Hospital and then caring for private patients in their homes. It was whilst doing so, probably in Southampton, that she read scandalous newspaper reports about the awful suffering of soldiers in the Crimea. She wrote a letter, which is now in the National Archive at Kew, volunteering for nursing service there. In her letter she says

> *My age 44 robust Constution and I will Indevour to do the utmost of my power to sirve the Sufferers in the War.*

Her letter contained one significant falsehood.

She lopped twenty years from her age. And by so doing, quite suddenly, at the age of 65, she entered the most significant part of her life.

As soon as she arrived in the Crimea, she knew she disliked Florence Nightingale intensely. The wounded were brought away from the front to Scutari where there were five miles of beds, all filled, and Nightingale would walk by them all every night, earning herself the name of *'The Lady with the Lamp.'*

But in Scutari, Betsi was a long way from the action and she became frustrated. Nightingale, however, refused to let her nurses go any nearer the front. It was far too dangerous and the front-line hospital was filthy and disorganised. Instead, the nurses were mending shirts and sorting through rotting linen. Nightingale was autocratic and domineering and a clash with the opinionated and frustrated Betsi was inevitable. The latter had come on a mission to care for the wounded and Nightingale seemed to be standing in her way. She let everyone know what she felt.

Florence described her as *'that wild woman from the Welsh Hills,'* and accused her of upsetting her other nurses through her insubordination. She threatened to send her home, forfeiting her pay. When she maintained her defiant opinions and said she was determined to make her own way to the front line in the Crimea, Nightingale washed her hands of her.

Betsi left and headed up to the front to the hospital at Balaclava. What she found there was truly horrific. *'I shall never forget the sights as long as I live,'* she said later. The first man she treated had frostbite. *'His toes fell off with the bandages. The hand of another fell off at the wrist.'* There were no beds. The men lay on boards, with their coats for pillows.

They were dirty and dying, their wounds had remained untreated for weeks at a time and were infested with maggots, which she removed by the handful.

She nursed these men for over six weeks before being put in charge of the kitchen. Her skills in domestic service were put to good use and she was skilled at foraging for food and for wasting nothing. It was at this basic level of individually focused care, that Betsi was determined to make an impact.

Betsi was a remarkable woman. Full of energy, certainty and opinions. She had no time for procedure and systems. She wanted only to give front-line care. Of such are heroines made. But without the proper structures, such care might remain unfocused and untargeted. It was easy for Betsi to pillory Florence Nightingale, but she gave the job of nursing a professional structure. She created order and systems to channel the emotion and compassion that fuelled Betsi. She on the other hand, was a practical person who had little time for 'management.' A true working-class hero, working amongst her own people. The point of course is, as a patient, who do you need at such times? A bum wiper or a file carrier?

She believed in manual labour to which *'high born gentlewomen'* like Nightingale were not suited. She believed that they

22

hurt the feelings of the men, who were acutely sensible of the unfitness of such work for persons of high station. Ladies may be fit to govern, but, for general service, persons of a different class, who could put their hands to anything, were more useful.

The world though, is rarely so simple. It was the work of Nightingale that ultimately made nursing an acceptable occupation. And it is to her credit that she came away from two visits to Balaclava with a changed impression of Betsi, even to the extent of recommending her for a government pension.

In 1855 Betsi returned home. Even though she was exhausted by over-work and by dysentery, she continued with her mission to blame Nightingale for the lack of direct patient care. But Betsi was largely unsuccessful, for the legend of Florence Nightingale was already starting to take hold.

Betsi was a girl for getting her hands dirty. Yet fame largely passed her by and it was Florence Nightingale who entered the national consciousness. Now, when Betsi is remembered, she is remembered as the *'Welsh Nursing Heroine.'* She certainly had admirable qualities. She was calm, ordered, compassionate. Betsi never embraced the deep despair that drove some of the other nurses to breaking point as they cared for destroyed and mangled bodies. She saw that something needed to be done, so she got on with it.

Both Betsi and Florence worked tremendously long hours, sometimes up to 20 hours a day for weeks at a time. But Florence had her own servants to look after her; Betsi did not. She cooked and she cleaned and she cared, fuelled only by her own personality and her determination. And at the age she was, she paid a heavy price.

She went to live with her sister Bridget in London and she died, forgotten and in poverty, in Shoreditch in the summer of 1860.

She is no longer forgotten entirely. Her name lives on in her local hospital trust. And an annual nursing lecture has been named in her honour in Cardiff. She is honoured for having *'advanced the cause of patient care.'* Because this is what she put first. She would accept nothing else and held Nightingale in contempt because of this.

Another Welsh woman too accompanied Nightingale to the Crimea – Jane Evans, known apparently, and unkindly, as 'Plain Jane from Caio.' She also was a practical nurse who acted as a chaplain at times and, like Betsi, altered her age. She was, in fact, fifty when she went out there. There is a plaque in her honour in the Presbyterian Chapel in Pumpsaint in Carmarthenshire.

Bodelwyddan, Denbighshire
Rebecca Macintosh, 1919

The Kinmel Park Camp Riot

It is such a distinctive church. It can be seen for miles, standing tall and pale on the coastal plain. It has an elegant limestone steeple in keeping with its beautiful interior. St Margaret's Church in Bodelwyddan, 'The Marble Church', is an impressive place. It has inside many different types of marble, including beautiful Belgian red marble in its pillars. The style and the decoration are enough to draw the visitor. But it has other interests too.

David Gillan's grave is in the centre

On the south side you will find a host of military graves. There are 34 British graves and then 83 graves of Canadian military personnel who had been stationed at the nearby military camp at Kinmel Park, outside Abergele. They have a memorial cross of red sandstone and their graves are grouped around it.

Our military heritage spreads far and wide, encompassing the legacy of empire and commonwealth. We must never forget that people from across the world have fought and died for us. And some of them rest with us still. Here in Bodelwyddan it is the children of Canadian mothers.

And as they have rested, rumours have grown up about these Canadian graves, rumours of riot and summary execution in the aftermath of war in March 1919. And the question has always been, why did these survivors of the Great War die in North Wales?

The Kinmel Park Camp near Abergele was built in 1914 as a training camp for the North Wales battalions and when the war ended it became a transit camp – a base for soldiers from across the Empire, waiting to go home. The 9th Canadian General Hospital was there too. It contained, in huts and under canvas, 1290 beds. It was a busy place.

In the late winter of 1919, the camp was dirty and over-crowded. The Canadian soldiers were on half rations. They hadn't been paid. 42 men lived in huts meant for 30. There was no coal for the stoves. There was a shortage of bedding and they took it in turns to sleep on the floor. March can be cold in North Wales.

They just wanted to be home, and four months after the end of the war very little progress was being made. There were over 15,000 of them and as far as they were concerned their military service was over.

Repeatedly they were processed and given a place on a ship, which then didn't turn up. Whilst they waited, they continued to live under military discipline, with drill, parades and forced marches. Local tradesmen who set up stores in adjacent shacks in what they called 'Tin Town', were felt to be profiteering, overcharging men who had little money in the first place.

There are always frustrations when you think you are in a queue and yet others seem to be dealt with first. Sometimes newly arrived troops appeared to be sent home before longer term residents.

Certainly, Kinmel Park camp was not a cheery place to be. Things back at home weren't ideal either, and the Canadians were not sure what they would find when they returned. Unemployment in Canada was widespread and the economy was crippled by war debt. Industrial unrest was growing and the Government was calling in the troops who had then started to fraternize with striking workers. Communists were a hidden, sinister threat, blamed for the unrest.

Canada was uneasy in the aftermath of the Russian Revolution. Overseas workers, generally Russian immigrants, were being deported to provide work for returning soldiers. But it offered little comfort, for many of them were of Russian descent themselves. This tension reached out across the Atlantic to North Wales.

Strikes at home had held up the repatriation ships. Promises that those who had enlisted first and married men would be sent home first, were not being fulfilled. They were probably being sent home by unit, rather than by date of enlistment. But it was certainly a big issue and the commander of the camp, Colonel Colquhoun, sent Colonel Thackrey to London to discuss the problem. Meanwhile the camp believed with absolute certainty that a troop ship intended for them had been diverted to Russia to carry grain.

Not only that, but Kinmel Park Camp was also a dangerous place to be. Soldiers were dying in the flu epidemic that had reached the camp in October 1918 and which would eventually account for the vast majority of the casualties now buried in the cemetery.

The 1918 flu pandemic (often called 'the Spanish flu') spread to nearly every part of the world. Unusually most of its victims were healthy young adults, those who had survived the Great War. The epidemic began in March 1918 and went on to kill anywhere between 2% to 5% of the human population. People could be apparently well, then suddenly overwhelmed by symptoms and then dead the following day. The flu provoked huge fear right across the world and the conditions in a place like Kinmel Park were ideal for the spread of the virus.

February 1919 was a particularly bad month, as the dates on the headstones testify. Kinmel Park Camp was clearly somewhere you would not wish to be.

It was inevitable that frustrations would eventually boil over.

The riot started on Tuesday 4 March 1919. A committee was formed with the intention of starting a mutiny that they hoped would spread through all the estimated 15,000 men. The leader of the action was identified as William W. Tarasevich of the Canadian Railway Troops. They began by ransacking the canteen and soon gangs were roaming round the camp, looking for other ways of expressing their anger.

They broke into the rooms of girls who worked at the camp but only to steal overalls. Then they moved on to Tin Town and smashed it up.

Colonel Colquhoun acted swiftly. He ordered all remaining beer to be poured away and all ammunition removed. He tried his best to calm events by moving about through the camp and speaking to the men. In so doing he managed to control the spread of the disorder through his presence. However, there is a suggestion that the rioters looted a brewer's dray on Wednesday morning when it turned up at the camp. *The Times* said that this *'may account for the horrible turn of events in the course of the afternoon.'*

On Wednesday afternoon there was a confrontation between the rioters and those who had remained loyal. Some soldiers on both sides had retained firearms and ammunition. Perhaps it was inevitable that they would be used. A shot was fired and Gunner Jack Hickman took a bullet the heart as he sat in his hut writing a letter home. Another four were killed in the hand-to-hand fighting that followed, including Tarasevich. Then, the riot was over.

Tarasevich was the perfect scapegoat. The rioters had already been described as '*not true Canadians but men with Russian blood*' and his death was especially convenient. Everyone could blame a dead man with a Russian name and then move on.

Official reports blamed Russian Communists for the riot. *The Times* says, '*in the camp itself there is a strong belief that Bolshevism tried to raise its head and was scotched,*' but the reporter himself was more circumspect.

> *To what extent the use of the red flag – it was a piece of bunting that had flown at a canteen – signified a political impulse behind this unhappy business it is difficult on present information to say with any confidence.*

What we do know is that those who died in the riot received a military funeral in St Margaret's, with six pall bearers, a firing party of twelve men, twenty-four mourners and a bugler. Hickman was taken home for burial but the other four are there.

Tarasevich, 30 years old, bayoneted in the abdomen.

Corporal Joseph Young, 36, an Infantryman in the Manitoba Regiment, who died in hospital after being hacked in the face with a bayonet.

Gunner William Haney, 22, of the Canadian Artillery, who was shot in the face.

Private David Gillan, also 22, of the Nova Scotia Regiment, was shot in the back of the neck. Gillan's memorial is a larger, private headstone. It reads, '*Killed at Kinmel Park on March 5, Defending the honor of his country.'*

Whilst it is believed that the first three were part of the riot, there was no distinction in death. Who can tell what small acts of heroism they had performed during their service in Europe? So, they are rightly buried together.

The unrest faded. General Sir Richard Turner VC, travelled from London and re-assured the troops that four transports to Canada would arrive as soon as possible. He acknowledged that there had been difficulties in shipping in February, but he hoped and promised that things would improve.

Of course, there had to be Court Martials and soldiers were sentenced and imprisoned, but they were soon quietly sent home along with their comrades.

There was some excitement in the press, which was probably the origin of all the myths about the riot that persist to this day.

The riot was carefully planned by Russian Communists, desperate to incite revolution. There have been stories of twelve officers being killed, of Irish Guards being sent in to quell the riots, of summary executions by firing squad, heard clearly by frightened locals, of twenty-one dead soldiers buried secretly in unmarked graves...

But there is no evidence at all for any of this. The Canadian National Defense Headquarters denies it all and the Military Court of Inquiry was quite clear in its careful narrative of these sad events.

Does St. Margaret's Church hold a terrible and sinister secret?

Probably not.

Certainly, a tension exists between the official version and an alternative oral tradition. But it is in the nature of conspiracy theories that they persist. They can give a seductive order to otherwise random events. Life however is generally far too untidy.

There were no mass executions in Kinmel Park. There was no revolutionary uprising that was brutally suppressed. Just a sudden eruption amongst men desperate to get home, men whose sensibilities had been coarsened by their experiences in the trenches and in a grim inhospitable camp, for whom life had a disturbing cheapness.

The truth is probably quite straightforward.

A frustrated, frightened group of soldiers, a long way from home, facing a silent invisible killer in the shape of influenza, living in dreadful conditions, exploited, cold and hungry, were incited to riot. For a brief moment disorder ruled amongst men with guns. And then the madness passed.

On Joseph Young's gravestone is the message: *'Sometime, sometime we'll understand.'* I hope that we do.

Perhaps in the end we need to look no further than the marble cross right at the end of the first row of graves.

In memory of Nursing Sister Rebecca Macintosh, died at Kinmel Park 7 March 1919. Aged 26 years.

Whilst the riot was going on, a member of the Canadian Medical corps was dying of 'flu in the hospital. That was the true killer in the camp. The soldiers had all been heroes, like all the ordinary men who fought in the war. Then they had fought each other in their fear and their frustration.

Those 83 graves in Bodelwyddan are not there because of an act of suppression and brutality. They are part of the damage of a global catastrophe.

Rebecca Macintosh, who died in the Spanish flu' epidemic

Brecon, Powys
Charles Lumley VC, 1858

Wounded at Sebastopol. Died in Brecon.

When I asked about the tomb in the Cathedral, no one seemed to know anything about it. Never really taken much notice of it, I suppose. Just one amongst many. But I found it in the graveyard, where the great and the good of Brecon were surrounded by the falling leaves of autumn.

It is a large and imposing tomb. Well proportioned. Solid. In its time it meant something. It was an acknowledgement of what he had done. Yet today it is neglected, ignored.

In the grounds of Brecon Cathedral

33

The children from the school, laughing their way along the path close by, were not much troubled by him at all. I watched them as they kicked through the leaves. They were concerned only for life, not for the death all around them, as they called to each other carelessly and made their way home through the grounds of Brecon Cathedral. And why shouldn't they? Their lives are in front of them; they have so much to look forward to.

Charles didn't feel that way. And there is something very affecting about the life and death of Charles Lumley, something that troubles me. For he tumbled into darkness. Charles Lumley, VC. An early victim of post-traumatic stress disorder.

There are life-changing moments for all of us, I think. The trick is recognising them; many of us don't know they've happened until it is too late. It was too late for Charles Lumley.

Charles Lumley was a military man. The details of his early life are sketchy and open to some debate, but the most reliable information would suggest that he was born in Kidbrooke in Kent around 1824, the son of a merchant. In 1841 he appears in the census as a gentleman cadet at the royal Military Academy in Woolwich and then, 10 years later, he is a soldier living with his mother at Shooters Hill. When he was married in 1852 to Letitia Beaulieu in Marylebone, he was described as a Lieutenant in the Army in the Earl of Ulster's Regiment. So far, so good. A career soldier, and in 1854 he was posted to the Crimea.

The Crimea was an awful place, a genuine fore-runner for the stalemate in the trenches of the First World War, just as bitterly cold, just as muddy and just as deadly. The triumphs of the Napoleonic wars were a distant memory. The army appeared incompetent and disorganised, particularly when compared to their allies, the well-provisioned and efficient French. The British soldiers felt neglected and forgotten. 5,000 of them died in battle but 16,000 died of diseases like cholera. Those great battles, remembered in the names of rows of terraced houses, like Alma,

Inkerman, Sebastopol, Balaklava were inconclusive.

But as always, amongst all this hopelessness and incompetence, there were individual acts of heroism which were recognised in the award of the newly created Victoria Cross, one of which was carried out by Charles Lumley.

The key strategic feature in the war was Sebastopol. To succeed the allies needed to take it from the Russians, but they had fortified the city and had strong defensive positions.

Whilst their trenches were slowly getting closer and closer to the city, the only way the allies could take it was in a direct frontal assault. After a bitterly cold and cruel winter, when an inadequately provisioned army had shivered and died, the time had come. 1855 was to be the year they were sure, for a quick and decisive victory, which would be inevitable once Sebastopol had been taken.

The British were to attack a defensive feature called the Redan, against which their efforts had been directed throughout the summer of 1855. The French were to attack a defensive redoubt called the Malakoff.

The Russians came under heavy bombardment for three days prior to the assault. Over 13,000 shells were fired, though to little effect. When the British troops launched their attack at dawn on 8 September 1855, the defences were still intact. The Russian fire was very heavy but British troops still managed to fight their way into the Redan using scaling ladders. The dead and wounded were falling down these ladders as others fought their way up, so it was impossible to get soldiers on to the Russian parapet in sufficient numbers.

One of the first officers into the Redan was Lieutenant Charles Lumley. As he reached the parapet, he could see three Russian gunners reloading their field gun. He attacked them single-handed.

You can read his citation for the Victoria Cross in the National Archive, as it appeared in the London Gazette in February 1857.

he…immediately engaged with three Russian gunners…he shot two of them with his revolver, when he was knocked down by a stone, which stunned him for a moment, but, on recovery, he drew his sword, and was in the act of cheering the men on, when he received a ball in the mouth, which wounded him most severely.

The stone that hit him was most likely to have been a handful of cannon shot, thrown by a desperate Russian who had no time to load his gun. It obviously worked, for it knocked Lumley to the ground. Perhaps it gave him time then to load his gun. The subsequent bullet in the mouth was, of course, most effective.

It was a severe wound, although not fatal, and he was taken back from the Redan to the British lines for treatment.

The rest of the troops withdrew in confusion, despite the best efforts of their officers to rally them, and the Russians held the Redan. The French attack on the Malakoff however, was successful, which did little for British morale.

Charles Lumley was sent home on 29 September 1855. It was up to others now to play out the final few months of stalemate.

Bravery and suffering cut little ice. Although Charles' actions had been recognised and he was promoted to major, he was still put on half-pay until he could find a new position. But, along with the others decorated for their heroism on that day at the Redan, Lumley attended the first VC investiture in Hyde Park in London on 26 June 1857. He was a hero just like the others. But his wound had changed him; he was a much-troubled man.

He was appointed to the 23rd Regiment of the Royal Welch Fusiliers in 1858 and was stationed in Brecon. The appointment did not prosper. He found the work difficult and felt that administrative duties prevented him from being an effective commanding officer. He became eccentric and hot-tempered. Matters suddenly came to a head on Sunday 17 October 1858.

He had had a difficult weekend. On the Saturday he had been behaving oddly. He called his adjutant Richard Davies to his room on a number of occasions, but each time there was nothing that he wanted. In the afternoon he and Letitia had planned to ride, but the groom was not available. He flew into an enormous rage. Later when Davies brought him tea, he refused to drink it and instead walked round and round the barrack square. He was still there when Davies went to bed at 10.00 pm.

On the Sunday morning he was still behaving oddly. Davies said later, '*He was looking at me in a very strange manner. His look that morning frightened me.*'

Mrs Lumley went off to church, as did Davies. Charles was not there when they returned. Letitia noticed that his pistol was missing. She sent Davies to look for him.

He didn't have to go far.

Lumley was in the toilet with the door closed, though not locked. He was lying on his left side, holding the pistol in his left hand. He had clearly turned his head to the left and shot himself '*two inches behind the right ear.*' A single pistol ball was recovered from his brain. Although he was not dead when Davies found him, he died a few hours later.

An inquest was held on the 25 October which decided that he had taken his life '*whilst labouring under temporary insanity*'. Obviously, his mind was disturbed. But the inquest couldn't work out why,

When you look at his story it is clear that the events at the Redan had changed him. A serious head wound had caused a black cloud to settle over Charles Lumley that would not go away.

He felt compelled to complete what the Russians had started three years before.

It is not only here in Wales that he is remembered. His name appears on Letitia's headstone in Bath, where she lived until she died in 1890. Her husband is still in Brecon, where he fell.

Charles Lumley VC was buried with full military honours in the churchyard of Brecon Cathedral. You will find his tomb quite easily if you look in the north east corner of the churchyard. Walk along the path that the children use and look up to the boundary wall.

Charles Lumley. Wounded at Sebastopol. Died in Brecon.

Burry Port, Carmarthenshire
Amelia Earhart. Declared deceased 1939

Dismembered and Devoured?

I can only show you some memorials – Cambria Books' expenses wouldn't stretch far enough to send me to find where she rests, even if we could be sure where it is. There isn't a grave, but then there isn't a body, for it might have been eaten by coconut crabs. Let us hope fervently that she died before they got to her.

In Wales we have things more solid by which we can remember Amelia Earhart. And they are in Burry Port in Carmarthenshire. Or alternatively there is one in Pwll, two miles away. There can be no compromise, no third way. Along the shore of Carmarthen Bay you are defined by the answer you give to this question; where exactly did Amelia Earhart land? Such a simple question and yet so very complicated.

Amelia Earhart was born into comfortable affluence in Atchison, Kansas in 1897 - her father was a lawyer and her grandfather a judge and president of a savings bank. It was, however, a troubled childhood and her early adult years were difficult too, as family finances crumbled. During the WW1 she worked as a nurse's aide in a military hospital in Canada and later became a social worker in Boston.

She was always unconventional, always looking for new challenges. It is interesting, I think, that she collected newspaper articles about women who succeeded in what were then considered to be male careers. And it was aviation that became her passion. She had her first lesson in January 1921 and within six months bought her first plane, which she used to set the women's altitude record.

In 1928, in response to her growing celebrity, she was invited to join pilot Wilmer Stultz and mechanic Louis Gordon on a transatlantic flight as a passenger. They left Trepassey Harbour in Newfoundland on 17 June for Southampton.

They arrived at Burry Port, Carmarthenshire 21 hours later, in a Fokker seaplane that was running out of fuel, convinced that they were landing in Southampton in time for a civic reception. Well, it's a mistake easily made. They had been flying through such fog and rain that they didn't see Ireland at all and were therefore a little disorientated.

Remembered in Pwll

Now, the people of Pwll claim they spoke to Amelia first, when she put her head out of the door of the seaplane and asked - '*Where am I?*' A boy on his way home from school for his dinner answered. '*You are in Pwll Slip,*', words which can unsettle even the most intrepid of travellers. It has to be acknowledged however, that everyone's uncle has subsequently been credited with those fateful words. The plane was then towed into Burry Port Harbour by Ossie Roberts from Pwll.

However, Burry Port insists that she shouted, '*Where am I?*' at Dai Harvey Thomas, who was fishing and approached the plane cautiously in his rowing boat. She was unable to understand a word he said, slammed the door in disgust and was towed in to Burry Port by Mr Fisher, the manager of the local Frickers Smelting Works. You know, the man who had the motorboat.

Remembered in Burry Port Harbour

This difference of opinion has simmered for over ninety years and shows no sign of diminishing at all. Everyone agrees that the

41

first woman to fly across the Atlantic set foot on land in Burry Port, but that was only because Burry Port has a harbour, something else that Pwll has never been happy about. So both places have a memorial, for it is undeniable that Amelia Earhart was brought across the Atlantic and touched down in Carmarthen Bay. It is just that Burry Port has two memorials. The name of the seaplane was '*Friendship*,' by the way.

When the crew returned to the United States, they enjoyed a ticker-tape welcome in Manhattan and went to a tea party with President Calvin Coolidge at the White House, a privilege no longer afforded to contemporary transatlantic passengers.

Amelia always acknowledged that '*Stultz did all the flying. I was just baggage, like a sack of potatoes. Maybe someday I will try it alone.*' She did too, in 1932, landing in a field near Derry in Northern Ireland, for which she was awarded the Distinguished Flying Cross and this time got to meet President Hoover.

She became an iconic figure, America's daring darling. Huge crowds came out to see her land after flights to Honolulu and to Mexico. In August 1928, Earhart has become the first woman to fly a return journey across America alone. '*Women,*' she said, '*like men, should try to do the impossible and when they fail, their failure should be a challenge to others.*'

She had started to see herself as a brand and that brand needed constant feeding. She had to keep herself in the public eye, with new challenges, new adventures. Celebrity endorsements helped her finance her flying, as did her appointment as an associate editor for *Cosmopolitan* magazine. Her husband, George Putnam, was a publisher and publicist and later an executive at Paramount Pictures. Soon a wide range of promotional items bearing her name appeared, including luggage, women's clothing and sportswear. It is interesting to note in the light of subsequent events, that she used her initials A.E as a brand name, for this was the name used by her family and friends.

But there was one challenge she was anxious to take on —to become the first woman to circumnavigate the globe in a plane. A Lockheed Electra was built specifically for her. Most of the cabin windows were removed since they were redundant; the fuselage was filled with extra fuel tanks. Her first attempt in March 1937 failed at an early stage in Hawaii, when the landing gear collapsed on take-off, so she tried again in June 1937. This time Amelia travelled east from California to Florida and then onwards to a whole host of exotic destinations – Khartoum, Calcutta, Rangoon, Singapore, a journey which included the thrills of dysentery and the worrying removal of parachutes in Darwin, Australia. She arrived with her navigator Fred Noonan in Lae, Papua New Guinea, after covering 22,000 miles. The remaining 7,000 miles would be over the Pacific and she took off on 29 June 1937. She was never seen again.

The next scheduled stop to refuel was a small uninhabited scrap of land, Howland Island, very small, very undistinguished but, helpfully, very flat. An American Navy vessel, the *Itasca* was sent there to guide the Electra into land by radio. But there were inadequacies in their radio communication and Earhart and Noonan do not seem to have seen the tiny island. The *Itasca* generated smoke from her boilers but they did not appear to see that either. The plane disappeared.

The search for the plane began within an hour and continued for two weeks but to no avail. It was felt that Amelia Earhart had run out of fuel and crashed into the sea. Of course, alternative theories still persist. One popular idea suggests that she was captured by the Japanese and imprisoned briefly on the island of Saipan, where she left her initials scratched into the wall and ceiling of her prison cell, before she was shot as a spy. Those initials, A.E. Straight lines. Easy to scratch into a wall, perhaps?

The most enduring version has Amelia and Fred landing on the exposed reef of Gardner Island in the western Pacific (now called Nikumaroro and today part of Kiribati) where they lived as castaways for a short period. For ten days or so, radio hams across the world claimed to have picked up uncorroborated messages from her. Eventually, debilitated and dehydrated, they were terrorised and then dismembered and devoured by fearsome coconut crabs.

Recent archaeological digs on the island have been inconclusive. A jar which may once have contained freckle cream might be significant evidence. Bones were found but then subsequently lost. But these could the legacy of a British project to establish a settlement there between 1938 and 1963, which failed due to a lack of fresh water.

Amelia Earhart and Fred Noonan were officially declared dead in their absence in January 1939.

She has left a legacy behind her as a pioneer and an adventurer, though for some her death is far more important than her life and there are obsessives everywhere who are convinced that they have solved the mystery of Amelia Earhart. But proper evidence is unlikely to emerge now – unless the remains of the plane suddenly emerge from the deep.

On the basis that common things are common, perhaps it is most likely that she couldn't find Howland Island and crashed into the hazy vastness of the Pacific when she ran out of fuel. Perhaps that is better to hold on to that idea, rather than think of poor Amelia being eaten alive by those coconut crabs with their monstrous claws.

Remembered in Burry Port

Capel Curig, Gwynedd
Alice Douglas-Pennant, 1939

Essere amato amando

Capel Curig sits on the A5, the road from London to Holyhead, and is one of the gateways to Snowdonia, a place loved by walkers and climbers. Typically, we were not there for the mountains and the rocks; it was St Julitta's Church and its fascinating graveyard that drew us there, to find Lady Alice Douglas Pennant.

At the crossroads take the A4086 and, as the road bends across the river, pull in on the left to the church. It is a peaceful place, the smallest church in Snowdonia. There was a memorial service for her, in Knightsbridge (naturally), but Alice was buried here, towards the back of the graveyard on the left, for this was a place she loved, a place full of memories of happy holidays.

St Julitta's in Capel Curig is a beautiful place

46

For some, her story is particularly moving, for it hints at the sadness of unfulfilled love, because of some words scratched on the window of her bedroom in Penrhyn Castle. It is said that Alice fell in love with a gardener in 1880 and was banished to the castle tower by her father as a punishment. She scratched her love on a window pane, and that message is still visible.

Lady Alice was born in Chesham Place in London in 1862, the daughter of George Sholton Gordon, the 2nd Baron Penrhyn of Llandegai. She was one of fifteen children brought up in Penrhyn, the neo-Norman castle in Bangor, between Snowdonia and Menai Strait. The extreme wealth of the Pennant family came from the sugar trade and their huge plantations in Jamaica, which were worked by enslaved people. The family were vociferous opponents of the abolition of slavery and they carried similar attitudes into their business in Wales. They developed the huge Penrhyn slate quarry at Bethesda, which at the time was the largest in the world. Lord Penrhyn opposed both the unionisation of the workforce and any improvement in their working conditions. He once told the workers that inhaling slate dust was good for them, despite high mortality rates.

There were bitter and lengthy strikes. One in 1896 lasted for eleven months and the other which began in 1900 lasted for three years, the longest industrial dispute in British history, bringing poverty to the people and desolation to Bethesda. Lady Alice Douglas Pennant's life, in contrast, was one of privilege and luxury.

Penrhyn Castle, built between 1822 and 1837 and incorporating parts of a medieval structure, still retains the extravagance which is so far removed from the working lives in both Jamaica and Bethesda that paid both for the building, and the fine collection of art it contained. It included work by Canaletto, Gainsborough, Rembrandt and Richard Wilson; Alice later painstakingly catalogued it all.

But it is unexpected graffiti that is her most lasting legacy. For many years those scratched words on the glass were believed to be in poor Latin – *essere amato amando*. In fact, it is Italian which translates as *to be loved, whilst loving*. The teenaged Alice is in the frame, so to speak, because she had previously scratched her name on a different rain- shrouded window above the gardens.

Once Alice had been presented to Queen Victoria at Buckingham Palace in February 1880 - her clothes described in detail in the press, along with her splendid hat *'featuring a plume of white ostrich feathers and a veil'* - she assumed the lifestyle of a conventional aristocrat, devoted to good works, with strong conservative values. Of course, she had all the accomplishments of her class. She painted attractive watercolours, she played the piano and performed recitations. She appeared on stage in an amateur theatrical performance at the Chester Music Hall in October 1900 to raise money for Lady Lansdowne's Fund for the Officers Branch of the Soldiers and Sailors Family Association. In 1905 she sang at her own fund- raising concerts in Penrhyn Castle to raise money for the Imperial Yeomanry Hospital.

Alice was always at meetings and committees. She opened fetes and bazaars, in aid of the Aberdaron Church restoration fund, for example, and the Bangor Railways Institute's annual horticultural show. She was President of both the Caernarfon Welsh Industries Association, and the Caernarfon Needlework Association. She was invited to present attendance awards at the Glanogwen Girls' School in Bethesda in 1899 as well as the prizes at the Bethesda Cycle Races in the same year. She helped at the Christmas Tree Tea Party at the Conwy Workhouse in 1895 at which *'juveniles were given oranges.'*

She vehemently opposed the Welsh Church Act of 1914 which separated the Church in Wales from the Church of England, which Conservatives like Alice saw as a Liberal, non-conformist plot led by Lloyd George. As it says on her memorial in Capel Curig, *'She faithfully defended the ancient church in Wales.'*

Alice became a devoted contributor to the war effort, helping to publicise the government's official pattern for the making of knitted belts for the troops. In a letter to the press she writes, *'Many women are wishing to set to work at once,'* to make them and then qualifies it to suggest that others might *'employ and pay women in need of work in making them.'* In 1916 Alice wrote to the North Wales Chronicle, urging the collection of sphagnum moss for use as a surgical dressing. She also promoted the idea of camp libraries, sending books to the front for the troops, feeling that Wales was not pulling its weight in donations and saying *'In many a home there is now a shelf or cup- board of story-books belonging to the boy who will never come home again; to what better use can they be put than to send them to help and cheer those who are following his glorious example?'* which, try as I might, I cannot see as anything other than a little insensitive.

She was happy to report in 1919 that *'the Queen has graciously accepted the first length of hand-woven tweed made (not in Scotland) by a disabled soldier. It is a thick white material made at the Cambrian Factory, Llanwrtyd Wells, at the Training Centre for Disabled Soldiers as hand-loom weavers'.* She went on, *'One hopes that many disabled men may find happy employment as hand-loom weavers. There is no reason why a man unable to work regular hours or endure indoor life should not have his loom, set up close by his home in a half-open hut such as are now often used for open-air cures. I remember once in Italy seeing a silk weaver's loom set up in a nice little shed looking on to his pretty garden.'* Well, if you must insist on being poor or disabled, at least you can do your best to look picturesque.

Her photograph shows an attractive, if austere woman, well dressed and prosperous, an unnaturally thin waist, drawn in presumably by a vicious corset, her hair dressed carefully in curls. She was clearly a society lady, at home in fashionable London and in grand houses, but it is that unexpected graffiti that has come to define her.

Was she a girl briefly forgetting her place in the world and so her Victorian father reminded her forcibly of her role and her duty? This might have given her the opportunity to play the part of the forlorn renaissance lover, trapped in a tower by a cruel father, losing herself in an imagined Pre-Raphaelite painting, enjoying all that delicious agony of a bored, frustrated teenager, watching her crush in the garden, imagined for a moment as a medieval knight.

What do I think? There is no suggestion of any romantic involvement in her subsequent life, no engagement and she was an eligible aristocratic lady, certainly a 'good match,' always a noted guest at balls and at the weddings of others. She was of marriageable age long before the pool of possible husbands was horribly decimated in the First World War. But it didn't happen and it could have done. There could be many reasons for that, which might be more convincing than doomed love. Perhaps we have turned it into a romantic tragedy to suit our own needs.

It was, of course, a privileged life, mapped out for the inquisitive in the Tatler magazine. Alice travelled for example to India in 1924 as a guest of Lady Rawlinson. Her final trip abroad was in March 1937 when she returned from a trip to the Holy Land and she last appears in the press later in October as a mourner at the funeral of the former Dean of York. After this she disappears completely from public view. She died in a London nursing home in March 1939, after a long illness. She was 76. In her will she left £5000 as a contribution to the on-going restoration work on the belfry of the Cloth Hall in Ypres. She also gave £500 towards the building of a memorial to the men of Bangor who fell in the Great War, including her brother.

Cardiff, The Metropolitan Cathedral
SS Arandora Star 1940

Detained, Interned, Drowned

There has been a long history of Italian families who came to Wales from the Apennine region of northern Italy, especially from the hilltop town of Bardi. They were economic migrants, escaping rural poverty in Italy and bringing Mediterranean colours and enterprise to the rainy South Wales valleys. All our communities had their own Italian families who made themselves a part of our way of life – the Berni Brothers from Merthyr Tydfil for example, touched all of us when they founded the legendary Berni Inn restaurant chain.

But in 1940 we betrayed them and tore the heart from a community that has still not forgotten their innocent men who died at sea on *SS Arandora Star*.

On 2nd July 2010, the seventieth anniversary of the disaster, the *Arandora Star* Memorial was unveiled in the Metropolitan Cathedral in the centre of Cardiff. There is a touching beauty about the work, created by Welsh-Italian artist Susanna Ciccotti and sculptor Ieuan Rees. On the right you can see the Madonna who cradles the ship close to her, one which now rests 2,000 metres down in the cold North Atlantic, a ship on which over 800 innocent men died.

On the left there is a list of names which, in happier times, would speak of fish and chips, ice cream and frothy coffee - Conti, Ferrari, Pompa, Sidoli, Rossi, Bombelli, the five members of the Rabaiotti family. The tragedy of this list is that today, it says something entirely different.

51

In the Metropolitan Cathedral in Cardiff

Because these men were suspected, detained, interned, drowned.

At the beginning of the war, all foreign nationals living in Britain were assessed according to their potential threat to security, and tribunals were set up by the Home Office to examine each individual case. Only one percent of almost 80,000 cases could be considered as high risk and therefore subject to internment.

Everything changed in June 1940. The Germans occupied the Channel Islands and Italy declared war on Britain and the tribunal system became irrelevant the moment Churchill called for the police to *'Collar the lot'*.

All Italian men aged between 18 and 70 were interned. No matter how long they had lived in the country, the possession of an Italian passport was enough. So there were indiscriminate arrests as the police scoured addresses and shopfronts, looking for Italian-sounding names. The great threat that chip shop owners, barbers, chefs, waiters and ice cream men represented was thus confronted head-on and they were gathered together in transit camps, prior to their transportation to internment camps in Canada and Australia.

Many were then taken to Liverpool where they boarded SS *Arandora Star*.

The ship had been launched in 1927 at the Cammel Laird Shipyard at Birkenhead for the Blue Star Line and became one of its most popular liners, complete with tennis court and swimming pool. At the start of the war, it was re-fitted and deployed to evacuate Allied troops from Norway, Brittany and then from Bayonne. Now it was sailing across the Atlantic, painted grey with plenty of barbed wire to stop passengers getting off too soon, but with no Red Cross displayed to show that it was not carrying soldiers.

There were plenty of passengers, with over 700 Italians and 500 Germans watched over by 200 military guards, and with 174 officers and men in the crew. They set off for Newfoundland, travelling unescorted and unmarked at the beginning of July 1940.

They never made it.

At dawn on 2 July 1940, seventy miles off the North Atlantic coast of Donegal, the German U-Boat U-47, commanded by Günther Prien, tracked the *Arandora Star*. He was coming to the end of his patrol and he watched the ship carefully, unsure what it was. But the ship was using an evasive sailing pattern and seemed to be defensively armed, which made it a legitimate target. So Prien fired his last remaining torpedo, which he believed was probably faulty.

It wasn't.

The torpedo exploded against *Arandora Star's* starboard side, flooding the engine room, killing all the engine room personnel and destroying turbines and generators. All lights and communications were disabled. At 7.20 am the *SS Arandora Star* rolled over and then, stern first, began a two-kilometre descent to the bottom of the Rockall Channel, with the captain and his senior officers still on the bridge.

The Canadian destroyer *HMCS St. Laurent* managed to rescue 850 survivors but at least 805 men were drowned - internees, guards, crew - the sea does not discriminate.

It was a cold place to die. In what might be the deepest irony, some of the victims' sons were fighting in the British armed forces. Gerald and Leslie DiMarco were in the RAF and the South Wales Borderers but their father Michele, who ran three ice cream parlours in Swansea, was on the ship and his body was never found. Giovanni Cavalli had been detained at his house in Neath, his binoculars and radio also taken, just in case he was planning to assist any invaders. His children watched him being taken away and never saw him again. Luigi and Joe Rossi had been arrested in their café in Swansea and, after the attack, jumped together into the deadly black oil which surrounded the ship. Joe supported Luigi in the water for eight hours but when they were eventually rescued Luigi was dead. And when every man died, a part of their families died too.

You will find all three of them – Giovanni, Luigi and Michele - on that list of shame in Cardiff Cathedral.

The *Glasgow Herald* spoke to a surviving crew member who said, *'We cursed the U-boat, but not so much as did the Germans and Italians on board, who were almost ferocious in their denunciation of this type of warfare.'* The paper went on to write about desperate scenes on board the ship, with craven hysterical Italians and bullying Germans forcing themselves into lifeboats and pushing others out, but this was simply war propaganda playing to perceived stereotypes. Those who were there remember things differently.

They remember the quiet dignity of doomed men helping each other and taking orders from a German naval captain, Otto

Burfeind, interned after scuttling his own vessel the SS *Adolph Woermann* in November 1939. He stayed aboard *Arandora Star* managing the evacuation, until the ship turned over and he became one of the casualties. There were so many others. The sea was an alien environment to the men from northern Italy and many were reluctant to throw themselves into the water. The elderly and the infirm trapped below deck never had a hope of making it to the lifeboats.

Those who survived the sinking were taken to Greenock in Scotland and put on another ship - the *Dunera* – and sent to Australia, a journey which took two months, in what were described as 'horrendous' conditions. There the men were held in internment camps before they returned to South Wales at the end of the war.

Some of those who were lost were brought by tide and current to Colonsay in the Hebrides where they were laid to rest. North-westerly gales in August washed hundreds of bodies on to Irish beaches. The remains of a lifeboat can still be seen where it washed up on the island of Mull.

There are a number of memorials across Europe, in Glasgow, Liverpool, Lucca and Barga. In Bardi, in North West Italy, there is an *Arandora Star* Chapel and here in Wales we have our dignified *Arandora Star* Memorial.

There are also individual gravestones where bodies came ashore. Impoverished communities, especially in Sligo and Donegal, showed huge nobility and compassion in dealing with the bodies of these strangers as they washed up on the north Atlantic coastline. But they could provide neither coffin nor headstones when they buried them.

Some graves of course are marked. There is one for Walfrido Sagramenti who had been working as a sous-chef at the Savoy Hotel in London. Perhaps he cooked for Churchill. It is possible - Churchill was a regular guest and he often took the war-time cabinet there for lunch. Walfrido now rests on Colonsay.

Günther Prien himself did not prosper. He had been awarded the Iron Cross for the daring sinking of *HMS Royal Oak* whilst at anchor in Scapa Flow. However, he and his ship went missing in March 1941. One of the most successful German U-boats of World War II was sunk at the Rockall Banks, close to where it had successfully attacked *SS Arandora Star*.

All the crew were lost.

The Science Museum, London

In an unexpected postscript to this story, we found a complete scale model of the *Arandora Star*. We took Bethan and Sam, two of our grandchildren, to the Science Museum in London, and found it on display in the gallery, *Making the Modern World*. It is a beautiful model, built by Cammel Laird themselves, which emphasises the sleek design. You are aware of just how large a vessel it was. This model was originally displayed in the Blue Star showrooms on Regent Street and it is definitely worth going to see.

It is regrettable, though, that the full story of the terrible end of the *Arandora Star* is not properly presented on the display. It was a beautiful ship, without doubt. But it was also a tragic one.

Cardiff, Cathays
Jacques de Guélis, 1945

Silenced?

Hidden away in a corner of the large Cathays Cemetery in Cardiff, you will find two gravestones sharing the same enclosure. One is a family memorial, a large and imposing white cross, and the other is a Commonwealth War Grave, apparently no different from so many others throughout the world. This one though, tells a remarkable story, a barely remembered tale from turbulent times. For this is the grave of Major Jacques de Guélis, MBE MC, an agent of the under-cover Special Operations Executive (SOE) during World War Two who, whilst investigating possible war crimes in 1945, may have been assassinated.

The family graves in Cathays Cemetery, Cardiff

The cross remembers the extended de Guélis family, one which came originally from the Loire valley and developed a profitable business exporting Welsh coal to Brittany. Jacques was born in 1907 to a wealthy and educated family which was always keen to promote Anglo-French understanding. His maternal grandfather was Paul Barbier, a professor at the University of South Wales. His paternal grandfather delivered lectures to the Cardiff Anglo-French Society on subjects such as the writer Maupassant and the Paris Commune. During the First World War his mother was active in the Belgian Soldiers Fund which supported families that had fled to Wales to escape the German advance.

Jacques was educated in Cardiff and then at Magdalen College in Oxford. He held dual nationality and worked in advertising in both London and Paris, using his bilingual skills to good effect. He also completed his National Service in the French Army in the 1930s.

When World War Two began, not long after his marriage, he joined the staff of Lord Gort, the commander of the ill-fated British Expeditionary Force as an interpreter and was successfully evacuated from Dunkirk in June 1940. Rather unkindly in my view, he was almost immediately returned to France via Cherbourg, this time to liaise with units which were still fighting or trying to escape. His fluency in French was, at times, a bit of a burden.

When France signed an Armistice with Germany in June 1940, de Guélis went into hiding in Marseilles and then returned to London, via the Pyrenees, Spain and Glasgow. In April 1941, he was recruited to the Special Operations Executive by Lewis Gielgud, the brother of John Gielgud, once again on the basis of his language ability. The SOE had been created to encourage underground resistance and carry out sabotage missions in Nazi-occupied Europe. Although officers in other units regarded its clandestine operations with considerable distaste, it was a vital part of Allied operations. It mobilized and organised resistance groups, supplying materials and training and providing wireless operators to liaise with London.

Jacques was initially involved in training wireless operators and considered far too important to be risked in overseas mission, but as the war progressed, such niceties were abandoned. He became a part of the feverish needs of wartime, sent to fight his war where it was always best never to be seen. On his first mission he was parachuted into Vichy France in August 1941, the part of the country that was initially unoccupied by German forces, although in reality its government led by Marshal Pétain enthusiastically supported Nazi policies.

De Guélis was dropped near Chateauroux with a number of important objectives. He had to look for suitable landing fields where the RAF could safely deliver agents and supplies, particularly in the south where the river Rhone met the Mediterranean. He was required to recruit more agents, channel money to existing networks and collect examples of important documentation so that false ones could be produced with accuracy back in London. He was also had to prepare the way for the arrival of Virginia Hall, an American-born operative who was to become the first permanent SOE agent in France. She was a colourful character, not least because she had lost the lower part of her left leg in a shooting accident. She couldn't use a parachute so was brought to France from Spain on a fishing boat. Nonetheless she was extremely effective and the Gestapo, who called her 'The Limping Lady,' regarded her as their most important target, although they never succeeded in finding her.

By September his first mission was complete and de Guélis was picked-up from a remote field by a small Lysander aircraft, the first time the SOE carried out such an exfiltration operation. Rather carelessly perhaps, after a tense and unexpected meeting with a gendarme who wanted to check his documents, de Guélis laid out the landing lights in the wrong field which meant that the plane became entangled with electrical cables. Nevertheless he was safely returned to London.

As a result of the success of this first mission he was awarded the MBE (military division) and next, in November 1942, he was then sent to lead SOE operations in Algeria. A year later he was transferred to Corsica to support an anti-German uprising by establishing and provisioning additional resistance groups. It wasn't long before the Germans withdrew from the island completely.

Much of his work now took place back in London, in training and in planning, particularly for the D Day landings, but his main contribution to the invasion involved further work overseas.

A month after D-Day, de Guélis parachuted into France to work with the Resistance in the Corrèze region in south west France, where he organised ambushes of German forces. These were especially disruptive, keeping significant German forces away from the battles in the north as they tried to control the growing insurrection. Once the resistance groups were joined by a team of French SAS troops, they achieved the complete liberation in the region.

But de Guélis' work was not yet done.

As the collapse of Germany accelerated in May 1945, he travelled across large parts of newly-liberated Europe to locate captured agents and make sure they were still safe. Significantly, he was also required to gather information on the conditions experienced by prisoners of war. When he arrived in Germany, his investigations became focussed on a number of concentration camps, including Flossenburg in Bavaria, where leading members of the German resistance to Hitler and an SOE agent, had been hurriedly executed just weeks before. There was plenty of important material to be gathered which would have considerable post-war significance.

Then, on 16 May 1945, de Guélis was involved in a car crash involving a vehicle driven by a German soldier who had served at Flossenburg. De Guélis was seriously injured. He was flown to a military hospital in Lichfield but died there in August 1945.

But his death has subsequently become shrouded in the mists of conspiracy. Was it merely an unfortunate accident, the sort of thing that can happen anywhere, at any time? Or was it a deliberate- and successful - attempt to silence him and prevent information about Flossenburg being used in the Nuremburg war crimes trials? Was de Guélis assassinated? Who can say? But as far as the significant evidence he must have gathered is concerned, it all appears to have been lost.

His wife, Beryl De Guélis, arranged for his body to be returned to Cardiff for burial and Major Jacques Vaillant de Guélis now lies close to his family. He is in the shade of tree, which is rather appropriate for a man who fought his own important war in the shadows. His achievements were significant and he was recognised by both the British and the French who awarded him the Croix de Guerre on three occasions.

You can find his grave if you enter Cathays Cemetery through the main entrance on Fair Oaks Road. He is in Section I, which is to the right of the main path. The grave is 22E. You may however prefer to download the excellent Cathays Heritage Trail map from the website of the Friends of Cathays Cemetery. Number 10 is the grave you are looking for, and there are many other fascinating memorials to distract you. But Major Vaillant is more than worthy of your attention.

Cilgerran, Pembrokeshire,
Thomas Phaer 1560

The Boke of Chyldren

There is a sense of ancient history about St. Llawddog's Church in Cilgerran. Of forgotten stories, of secrets.

To find Cilgerran you should leave Cardigan on the A478 towards Narberth and turn left into the town. It is a pretty place, with a dominant and picturesque Norman castle standing above the Teifi. It has always been an important market centre, gathered tightly about the protecting castle. Today tourists come and enjoy the coracles and the atmosphere of a small town connected to its past.

As you enter High Street, turn immediately to the left and follow the road round and down, and it will bring you to the church of St. Llawddog. It is surprisingly well ordered. The churchyard has been tidied considerably and the stones in the older part placed in neat rows. This happened during restoration work in 1836 when, sadly, Thomas Phaer's grave disappeared.

There was a lot of tidying to do. The building had been there for a long time and had become dilapidated. The church was probably there in the 6th century and the earliest written record about it is from 1291. It is a church that Thomas would have known very well and it is where his gravestone was once a notable feature.

Another older stone was preserved, however. A megalithic standing stone is here, upon which Ogham script was carved. There are short and long notches along the edge, a form of writing used by the Irish and dating back to the 6th century. They were often erected over the graves of chieftains. This one says

'Here lies Trenegussus, son of Macutrenus.'

Turn left outside the vestry and you will see it, standing like a piece of rock that has fallen randomly from the sky, in the second row. It has an air of mystery. It makes you feel quite small to confront such a message from so long ago.

We were there in search of Thomas Phaer. Writer, magistrate, customs searcher and Commissioner for Piracy. Oh yes, he packed a lot into his fifty years. And he should be remembered not only for these things but most importantly for his work, *'The Boke of Chyldren,'* the first book in English on childcare.

There is a memorial to him on the left-hand side on the wall of the church as you approach the altar. It carries a quotation explaining why he wrote it.

Thomas Phaer MD of Cilgerran 1510 - 1560
Author of the first work in English
on child care.

To do them good that have most need
That is to say children
And to shew the remedies
That God hath created for the use of man.

The plaque represents an apology for the disappearance of his tomb and was installed as a result of donations from national and international medical societies. Because Thomas Phaer is a very significant figure, a pioneer of paediatric medicine.

The memorial plaque in St. Llawddog's Church, Cilgerran

It is hard to piece together accurate details of a life lived long ago which was largely unrecorded. But we do have some significant details. He was born in Norwich, perhaps in 1510, to Thomas and Clara. The family had Flemish origins. He was a highly educated man, attending Oxford University and then Lincoln's Inn. He followed a highly successful legal career. The key moment in his life was when he became Solicitor to the Council of the Marches and settled in Cilgerran. He married Anne, daughter of Alderman Thomas Walter of Carmarthen and lived at Fforest farm where they had three daughters, Eleanor, Mary and Elizabeth. Thomas was a JP and a member of Parliament for Cardigan. and he devoted himself to his extensive official duties.

In 1551 he surveyed the coast of Wales for Edward VI. He wrote *'all along this coast is no trade of merchandise but all full of rocks and danger.'* We should not forget that West Wales was an isolated and largely unknown place at this time. He became Customs Searcher and later Commissioner for Piracy. Because no matter how wild west Wales appeared, there were always those ready to exploit its remoteness.

But he combined his work with other things, particularly with writing. His first book was a legal work and he was also known as a highly regarded translator. He was especially well known for his translation of Virgil's '*Aeneid*', which remained the standard version of the text for almost 150 years.

Perhaps it was this interest in translating ancient texts that inspired the medical writing upon which his reputation has been based. Medical practise then relied upon ancient texts written by Galen and Avicenna and had thus remained unchanged for some considerable time. Thomas Phaer translated a poem called '*Regimen Sanitatis Salernitanus*', which was, unusually, a medical poem, written in this form to make it easy to memorise. He called his translation '*The Regiment of Life*' and in 1545 he published an addition to the work which was called '*The Boke of Chyldren.*' This was a highly significant moment and the book became extremely popular, running to several editions until 1596. It contains 40 diseases with '*remedyes*' in each case, including '*bredyng of teeth*' and '*pyssyng in bed.*'

The book recognises children as special class of patients, often ones who cannot explain precisely their symptoms and he makes a clear distinction between adulthood and childhood.

He considers '*manye grievous and perilous diseases*' in his book. So you will find references to '*apostume of the brayne*' (meningitis) and '*terrible dreames and feare in the slepe.*' (nightmares).

In 1559 he was awarded a Bachelor of Medicine Degree from Oxford and then a Doctorate, after having practised medicine, by his own admission, for twenty years. That level of experience is underlined by the strong thread of practicality that runs through his book.

Of course, some of what he writes is rooted very much in the times that he lived and opens a fascinating window on his world. In this way, it is a valuable record of social history.

For example, he says *'Stifnes of limes which thing procedeth many tymes of cold, as when a chylde is found in the frost, or in the street, cast away by a wyked mother.'* And whilst accidents in the home are as important now as they were then, few of us today would say that the major cause of ulceration of the head is from sides of bacon or salt beef falling from hooks in the ceiling.

As we can see, Thomas Phaer was writing at a time before spelling became standardised. You can see this in the different versions of his own name. Is it Phayer? Or Phaer? Or Phaire? There is certainly great pleasure in reading what he has to say because it seems so quaint. But never under-estimate the informed good sense that his words contain. He speaks for example about how parents should avoid elaborate cures.

'Of small pockes and measilles the best and most sure helpe in this case is not to meddle with anye kynde of medicines but to let nature work her operacion.' This is obviously not something that doctors would like to hear but it was undoubtedly the best advice available at the time.

His book contains references to antibiotics made from mould, using *'the musherom called iewes eares.'* He includes several medicines to kill lice, including *'Take mustered and dissolve it in vinegre with a lytle salt peter, and anoint the place where as the lyce are wonte to breede.'* There are some modern sounding practices too.

He writes about postural drainage. *'Of the cough it is good nowe and than to presse his tong with your finger, holding downe hys head that the reumes may issue…'*

Part of his mission was his desire to make medical advice accessible, to move away from the Latin that was normally used to obscure and to preserve a mystique. This is clearly why his work was such a popular one. He offered re-assurance and knowledge to parents who, just like ourselves, would suffer serious anxiety whenever one of their children was unwell. It goes to show that whilst times change, people stay very much the same. He was a great and influential man and it is such a pity that we no longer have his grave to honour.

But you may yourself have honoured him, perhaps unwittingly, if you have ever used his most famous sentence yourself.

'The eyes are the windows of the soul,' belongs to Thomas Phaer.

When Thomas died, in the autumn of 1560, his neighbour George Owen said of him that he was a *'man honoured for his learninge, commended for his governmente, and beloved for his pleasant natural conceiptes.'* We remember him still 500 years after his death, a sure sign of the great influence his productive life had upon others.

Clyro, Powys

Francis Kilvert,1879
Buried in St Andrew's Church Bredwardine, Shropshire.

Through an Enchanted Land

Clyro is such a peaceful place. The traffic rumbles along the A438 on the edge of the village but the untroubled churchyard is a tranquil haven. You can imagine Francis Kilvert sitting next to you on his favourite old tomb next to one of the splendid yew trees, and enjoying together the beauty of the hills where he walked and observed his parish. In his famous diaries he recorded an intimate picture of village life and captured the essence of the lost world of the Victorian countryside which has been matched only by the work of Thomas Hardy.

His grave in Bredwardine

Francis Kilvert was born in Chippenham, attended Wadham College at Oxford and then began his work in the Church of England as a curate in Clyro, a short distance from Hay on Wye, between 1865 and 1872. It was probably the happiest time of his life. He later served as vicar of St Harmon, Radnorshire, before his last post as vicar of Bredwardine in Herefordshire.

Kilvert was tall and bearded and regarded as being like '*a nice Newfoundland dog.*' He was a modest and naïve young man, rather innocent really, but he soon learnt the unexpected aspects of life in Radnorshire. He was once shocked to find a local clergyman's daughters helping to castrate lambs. Generally though, he was as comfortable with the poor as he was enjoying the picnics and the croquet and archery parties of the wealthy. Not everything was quite as idyllic as taking tea on the lawn though. He writes of poverty and mental illness, of murder and suicide.

He spent a great deal of time walking through the exquisite countryside where '*every step was through an enchanted land,*' visiting his parishioners and recording his life in spidery handwriting in his diaries. He reflects on the people he meets, many of whom seemed to be living a life from a different century.

Victorian London might well have been embracing the Industrial Revolution but Kilvert's parishioners would avoid a pond where they might be led astray by the Goblin Lantern. They told their boys to wear their hats the wrong way round so that they were not enticed into fairy rings and made to dance. To discover the name of a thief, one family confidently believed they should wrap a toad, together with a piece of paper, inside a ball of clay which should then be boiled or roasted. The toad would then obligingly scratch the name of the thief on the paper. Oddly, modern policing seems depressingly comfortable with a more technological approach to investigation.

Kilvert wrote about Mrs Sylvester, who villagers believed was the Woman Frog. They were absolutely convinced she had the legs and feet of a frog which she concealed beneath long dresses. She rarely went outside, apart from visiting the Primitive Methodist Chapel in Presteigne, conclusive proof indeed. It was an insular world too. His parishioners believed that it was impossible for him to travel from Clyro to Wiltshire without crossing the sea.

Kilvert found young girls attractive with the sort of enthusiasm which can make you uneasy and he kept falling in love with their older sisters. Daisy, Kathleen and Ettie are all significant figures in the diaries, but his romantic dreams never prospered. The end of his relationship with Ettie Brown in 1876 had a profound effect upon him. Some have speculated that the eighteen-month gap in the diaries indicates a period of severe depression. You begin to see the intrusive presence of illness and a fear of early death when his writing resumes. He once imagined skeletons in his room and his final poem, written at the end of May 1879, tells us that his *songs will soon be o'er.'*

In August 1879 he married Elizabeth Rowland but, just five weeks after their marriage, he died of peritonitis. He was 38. He is buried in the peaceful grounds of the Church of St Andrew in Bredwardine and there is a plaque in his memory in Saint Michael and All Angels, the parish church of Clyro.

There is a feeling of sadness when you consider Francis Kilvert's short life, which in some ways was sadly unfulfilled. He seems incomplete, frozen in time like an insect in amber, and perhaps like the world he described. He was always disappointed that his poetry never interested a publisher but did begin to think his diaries *'may amuse and interest some who come after me.'* He has certainly left behind a remarkable legacy.

All we can read however is a fragment of what Kilvert wrote. The diaries originally stretched from January 1870 to his death in September 1879, during which time it is believed that he filled 29 notebooks. His widow, Elizabeth, destroyed a number of them, removing all references to herself. The remaining diaries stayed within the family until they came to the attention of the author William Plomer, who prepared them for publication. The first volume appeared in 1938 followed by a second a year later and a third in 1940.

The books were tremendously popular, re-opening a door to the pastoral simplicity of a life still just within living memory, a time of peace and order suddenly swamped by the terrors of war. But the war had not only destroyed that lost world, but also wanted to keep its virtues hidden.

In wartime there was no paper available on which to print any more extracts. So there was a delay in the preparation of further volumes and in a terrible, irresponsible moment, Kilvert's elderly niece, who had possession of the diaries, destroyed them because they contained private family matters. It remains a deeply regrettable act of wanton destruction. Sometimes less is indeed more, but when you read his work, you always feel that it ends much too soon.

Ashbrook House where Kilvert lived in Clyro

He lived in Ashbrook House in Clyro which became, for a time, a respected art gallery but which at the time of writing stands empty. On the other side of the road you can see *The Baskerville Arms* which he knew as *The Swan* and where raucous drinkers would often disturb his summer evenings. He writes of easy summer days *'burning hot, sitting under the linden, reading'* or watching a solitary fern cutter at work on Vicar's Hill, but for me it is the winter sections that are the most notable.

Kilvert vividly describes a climate we no longer experience. In February 1870 there were few people in church because the weather was fearful, with a *'violent deadly east wind.'* His whiskers were *'so stiff with ice that I could hardly open my mouth and my beard was frozen on to my mackintosh.'* He conducted a baptism when the frozen water in the font had to be broken and the poor baby was surrounded by lumps of ice.

There were pleasures too, of course. People regularly went skating on iced ponds and rivers, with bonfires on the banks and with bands playing, the whole scene illuminated by Chinese lanterns, whilst children played on ice slides under bright star-filled skies. However, the shadow of danger was ever-present. Kilvert reported that the organist at Calne in Wiltshire fell on ice and broke his nose. The following day, his fifteen-year-old son fell whilst sliding on the ice, hit his head and died. Of course, for many, these days were hard indeed. Men would beat the holly bushes to flush out blackbirds to feed their families.

His description of Christmas Day in Clyro in 1870 is particularly eye-watering. There was an intense frost on Christmas Eve and when he climbed in his bath in his room in the morning, he found himself sitting on a sheet of thick ice. It broke into large pieces with *'sharp points and jagged edges'* all around the sides of the bathtub. He writes, rather phlegmatically, that *'it was not especially comforting'* to the naked thighs and loins.

'The keen ice cut like broken glass. The ice water stung and scorched like

fire. I had to collect the floating pieces of ice and pile them on a chair before I could use the sponge and then I had to thaw the sponge in my hands for it was a mass of ice.'

Thankfully, Francis Kilvert had his reward for such bravery. As he walked to the Sunday School *'the road sparkled with millions of rainbows, the seven colours gleaming in every glittering point of hoar frost.'*

It is like a traditional Christmas card made real, and Frances Kilvert's diaries, however incomplete they are, are a wonderful representation of that vanished world.

Dolgarrog, Conwy
Stanley Taylor, 1925

The Dolgarrog Dam Disaster of 1925

For us, this story started with a gravestone in the cemetery of St Tudno's Church on the Great Orme in Llandudno. It was a little faded in places but still bright in the sunshine, the details of a lost story set against a blue sky. Inevitably, for us it was a beginning of a search, but we could never forget that for a young family, the gravestone represented a tragic ending.

John Stanley Taylor, 29 years old, Dorothy Buddug his wife, 24 years, Sylvia Doris, their daughter, aged 17 months who lost their lives in the Dolgarrog Disaster on November 2nd 1925. The Lord gave and the Lord hath taken away. Blessed be the name of the Lord.

The Taylor grave in Llandudno

75

We could find no comfort in those words. We could not simply see that grave and walk away, we could not abandon Stanley and Dorothy and little Sylvia Doris. And so we found ourselves compelled to investigate the awful Dolgarrog disaster of 1925 and the death of a family in the November darkness of the Conwy valley, their small house on Machno Terrace devastated when two dams burst in the hills above and sent a torrent of water and boulders crashing down to devastate their home.

Dolgarrog is between Conwy and Llanrwst on the B5106, which runs along the west side of the Afon Conwy, and has an unexpected industrial heritage. In 1907 aluminium production began in a factory in the village, with water from dams in Snowdonia providing hydro-electricity. The business was successful and in 1916 a rolling mill was added, increasing their need for electricity. So the Aluminium Corporation decided to generate electricity themselves and constructed two dams in the hills, the Eigau and the Coedty, to power their own hydro-electric plant, situated next to the aluminium works. The dams, though, were not well made.

The flooding was triggered by a failure of the Eigiau Dam, which was breached following two weeks of heavy rain. At about 20:45, the water from the dam flooded downstream, into the Coedty dam, which was already full. Inevitably this dam also failed. When it collapsed, the thunderous sound echoed along the Conwy valley down to Llanrwst, and the combined contents, estimated at over 70 billion gallons of water and debris, which included enormous boulders, swept unchecked into Dolgarrog.

The wife of the manager of the Porth Llwyd Hotel thought that she should telephone the aluminium works to tell them that there was some water across the road but it did not appear to be especially serious. A few minutes later she called them again, this time to say that the annexe of the hotel had been swept away. It is an indication of how very quickly the disaster happened. In less than half an hour the houses on Machno Terrace, where the Taylor family lived, had gone. Here eight residents died. The church bell managed to ring three times in warning, before it was silenced and the building destroyed. Reverend Evans, who, ironically, had earlier given a sermon on the importance of being prepared, ran through the village warning residents but soon the church house, the sweet shop, Tai'r Felin, and the butcher's had also disappeared. Evans later rescued a young girl trapped on the roof of her house.

The flood killed 10 adults and six children. It could have been more but many of the residents were attending a film show in the village theatre, fortuitously situated on higher ground. Nevertheless, lives, and the community, were changed forever. it was a tragedy that took families. Three generations died in one house – Margaret Sinnot, her daughter Catherine McKenzie and her granddaughter Mona – though the family dog in an upstairs bedroom survived. Fred Brown, who lived long enough to become the last remaining survivor of the flood, was fourteen when the waters came, claiming the lives of his mother, Elizabeth, and younger sister, Betty. His father and his elder sister had also been washed away but managed to survive by crawling over coke wagons to safety. The next day he cycled frantically around the area searching for news of his mother.

The Memorial in Dolgarrog

77

This was a terrible tragedy amongst blameless, ordinary people. The list of victims includes Susana Evans and three of her children, Ceridwen, Bessie and Gwen, taken without warning. Cows were seen hanging from the trees and the aluminium works were submerged under 5ft of mud, but the 200 or so workers there were all successfully rescued. The hot furnaces exploded when they were inundated by the flood.

The jury at an inquest into those who died at Dolgarrog returned a verdict of 'accidental death', despite evidence which suggested that the dam wall had burst because of inadequately constructed foundations. At least the investigation led to improved construction requirements for dams in the UK, as part of the Reservoirs (Safety Provisions) Act in 1930, but for the village it was too late.

If you go up to Llyn Eigiau, in the hills above the village, you can still see the gap in the dam wall, like a careless gap in a giant's dentures, through which death poured unchecked. Today there is no one left who lived through that terrifying night and the only building left standing from the old village is the now-empty Porth Llwyd Hotel, but the residents are still anxious to honour those who died and have preserved the memory of a disaster that should never have happened. They have a small display of photographs and newspaper clippings from the disaster, with plans to set up a permanent museum in the community centre.

A pleasant Memorial Walk through the woods was opened in 2004. It was opened by the last survivor of the dam disaster, Fred Brown, with a disturbing soundtrack provided by the tumbling river. There is a plaque with the names of those who were lost and the walk traces the route the water followed, down which the water rushed to the village. You can walk amongst the menacing boulders brought down from the damaged dam and there are instructive panels outlining what happened. But it is the chilling enormity of the rocks that rest there where they were deposited, which will draw your eyes. The monumental legacy of the boulder field is something you will be unable to forget. Some of them are estimated to weigh in excess of 500 tons. When you look at them and consider the power of the water that moved them you could never underestimate the tragedy that they brought here.

If you search diligently on the website of the British Film Institute you will find a film taken by a local camera man in the days immediately after the catastrophe. There is still water flowing through the gap in the dam wall, even after the land has been scoured and drowned. There are broken houses in a featureless world, with their meagre contents desperately recovered and left outside on rocks, in the vain hope that they might one day be dry. You can see no trees, nor grass, nor fields. Just bewildered residents, mud, boulders and dirty water, making its inexorable progress to the river Conwy.

Some of the monstrous rubble washed down when the dam broke

It may not surprise you to learn that such was the interest in the disaster that police had to erect a roadblock to keep back crowds of onlookers obstructing relief operations, eager to see how the people of the village had suffered, for their own amusement. The film shows smartly-dressed female visitors in sensible boots, smiling as they are helped to step through the debris and the water using corrugated iron sheets as stepping stones, here in a village where children had died.

And what of that gravestone on the Great Orme? Stanley Taylor, 29-year-old, was at a Scouts meeting when the flood hit his family home on Machno Terrace. He died trying in vain to rescue Dorothy and Sylvia Doris from the wreckage of their home. During the First World War, Stan had served as a young soldier with the artillery on the Western Front surviving one disaster only to lose his life in another. Dorothy's father was a Llandudno journalist and historian, Arthur Richard Hughes, who was obliged by a terrible twist of faith to report on the disaster in which he had lost his daughter and her family.

They now rest together on the Great Orme, looking out towards the sea and those occasional blue skies, facing away from those dark treacherous hills in which their future together disappeared under the enormous rocks and in the cold impassive water.

Fishguard, Pembrokeshire
Jemima Nicholas, 1832

We'd have stayed at home if we'd only known...

Jemima has passed into Welsh mythology. The archetypal Welsh Mam. You love your Mam and respect her, but you mess with her at your peril. She runs the home and she runs your life and woe betide a troop of foreign soldiers who seem determined to upset her day. French soldiers land, they march, they get drunk and they are captured by a Welsh lady in a hat - Jemima Nicholas. She had better things to do in February than to be invaded.

Jemima remembered

She has come to represent this last invasion of the British Isles, even though she played a minor part in the events. But it was her contribution that turned this story of incompetence into a myth.

And really it all started with Napoleon. He was away campaigning in Central Europe and the revolutionary government, The Directory, devised a scheme to de-stabilise their enemy, England, by invading Ireland. At the same time, they would encourage the English to rise up against their oppressors and thus emulate the French Revolution. This would effectively neutralise British forces, which would become pre-occupied with maintaining order at home and consequently find themselves unable to fight in Europe. They would achieve this by landing troops in the North East which would march across the country to Lancashire, where they would meet up with a smaller force that had landed, either at Bristol or in Cardigan Bay, and then marched up in triumph to Liverpool. The population would be liberated and rise up in gratitude.

The reality was not so straightforward. The Irish invasion in December 1796 stalled due to bad weather and the fleet returned to port. The attempt to invade in the north was also abandoned. Despite this, inexplicably, the assault in the southwest still went ahead.

The leader of the expedition was an American of Irish descent, Colonel William Tate. He was 70 years old. His troops were a peculiar ragbag of deserters and royalist prisoners. Many joined straight from prison and some still wore the remains of their wrist and ankle irons. There were 1400 of them and they were dressed in captured British uniforms which had been inexpertly dyed to a patchy and mottled black. They were thus known as La Legion Noire. Tate himself spoke little French and relied upon three Irish officers to translate for him. Their mission, to blaze a revolutionary trail through Wales, was always going to be a challenge.

They embarked on four ships and spent a day or so flying a Russian flag and harassing small craft around Lundy, whilst waiting for the tide to carry them to Bristol. However, the winds were contrary so they headed off to West Wales instead. It could be no surprise that their presence in the Bristol Channel had warned the coastal defences, who were consequently on the look-out for them. Shots were fired at them near Ilfracombe, but they sailed on.

The weather was good for February as the four ships, flying British flags, sailed serenely into Fishguard Bay. That was probably the only thing that ever went to plan.

The defenders of Fishguard, positioned in a fort on the harbour, fired a blank shot from their cannon. It was either a customary greeting for an arriving English vessel or it was intended to warn the locals of danger. But it had the effect of making the French withdraw to anchor off Carreg Wastad, a rocky headland three miles west of Fishguard. It is a beautiful place but rather remote and inaccessible.

By 2.00 am on Thursday 23 February 1797 the invaders were ashore. Seventeen boat-loads of soldiers, forty-seven barrels of gunpowder and fifty tons of ammunition were all resting safely on a Welsh beach. It was quite an achievement in the dead of night. However, the terrain they encountered was especially unhelpful, with a stiff climb up from the beach to the headland. It must have been extremely hard work. A company moved inland and took possession of Tre Howel Farm, the most prominent building they could see, which Tate would use as his headquarters. Their job done, the ships sailed off and a sense of isolation and anxiety descended upon the invaders. Their escape route had disappeared over the horizon under full sail. Some of them had spent years on prison rations and began to pillage the area for food, chasing sheep and chickens. They are said to have looted an ancient chalice from the church in Llanwnda. They found a horde of port that the locals had salvaged from a recent wreck and very soon drunkenness and indiscipline settled upon them.

By morning, frightened soldiers, alone in a foreign land, began to threaten their officers. It was becoming clear too, that far from welcoming them with open arms, the Welsh were particularly hostile. As the day wore on there were deaths on both sides in a series of clashes.

The defending forces were all volunteers and they gathered slowly together from across west Wales. The militia, press gangs, sailors and civilians made their way towards Fishguard, whilst wealthier civilians fled in the opposite direction. The local forces, led by Lord Cawdor, were heavily outnumbered and they had fewer arms than the French. They carried spades, billhooks, scythes. Lead was stripped from the roof of Saint David's Cathedral to make bullets. Cannon were unloaded from ships in Haverfordwest and pulled along in carts. By early evening they were outside Fishguard, ready to attack what they believed was an overwhelming force of highly experienced professionals. Of course, the reality was entirely different.

By the end of Thursday Tate knew that all was lost. His troops were either drunk, asleep or in a state of mutiny. The farmhouse had been comprehensively trashed. There were bullet holes in the grandfather clock when drunken soldiers had fired at those supposedly hiding within. All food had gone, the window frames had been used as firewood.

That evening two delegates sent by Tate, rode down the steep roads and arrived at the Royal Oak Inn in Fishguard to negotiate, but Cawdor would only accept an unconditional surrender, on the basis of the complete lie that he was in command of superior forces. He gave them until 10.00 am on Friday to surrender or they would be attacked.

Tate's position was untenable. The Legion Noire had become a rabble and he believed that the countryside was crawling with uniformed defenders. At 2.00 pm on Friday the French marched down to Goodwick Beach where they stacked their weapons. They were taken away to temporary imprisonment in Haverfordwest. A small group of them later escaped and stole Lord Cawdor's yacht and sailed to France. Tate surrendered to Cawdor in the farmhouse and, after a period of imprisonment in Portsmouth, he was returned to France in a prisoner exchange in 1798.

The Royal Oak, Fishguard

Over time, mythology has taken hold and a cobbler called Jemima Nicholas from Main Street in Fishguard has become the central figure in the story. You see, there is some evidence that the French were deceived by the number of women in the neighbourhood wearing traditional dress – a red shawl and tall black hats which, from a distance, resembled infantry uniforms. And the story is that Jemima captured a dozen forlorn French soldiers by threatening them with her pitchfork and imprisoning them in St. Mary's Church. Depending upon which version you believe, she either found them in a field at Llanwnda or they walked straight into her in a narrow alley in the town.

Jemima was born in Mathry in March 1755, making her 41 at the time the invasion, which is close to contemporary accounts that put her at 47. We know little else about her. She was a cobbler or a shoemaker and she was buried in St. Mary's on 16 July 1832. She was clearly a formidable character around whom the legend gathered and settled.

Samuel Fenton, the vicar of St. Mary's in 1832, wrote on her burial record that she had '*such personal powers as to be able to overcome most men in a fight.*' A member of the Fishguard volunteers, H. L. Williams, writing in 1842, described her as '*An heroic single woman.*'

On her approach she saw about twelve Frenchmen; undaunted she advanced to them, and whether alarmed at her courage, or persuaded by her, she conducted them to, and confined them in, the guard house in Fishguard Church

Contemporary reports make no reference at all to the role of women in the action, though that may or may not be significant. According to these sources, it was Lord Cawdor and his irregulars who saved the day. There is no evidence, either, to support the tradition that Jemima was awarded an annual pension for life.

Today it is Jemima who is remembered. In Fishguard you will find a memorial gravestone, against the wall of St. Mary's church, raised by subscription at a banquet to mark the centenary of the invasion in 1897. And the event is remembered too by a solitary memorial stone high on the cliffs at Carreg Wastad that you can reach from the Coastal Path. She herself has slipped quietly back into history. Jemima Fawr. Jemima the Great. What she has become is a symbol of the indomitable Welsh woman, fiercely protective and ready to fight for her own, the one person even the most unsophisticated rugby player would not confront - Mam.

And yet there are no records to suggest that this most legendary of Welsh Mams ever married or indeed ever had children. But in the end, I don't suppose this matters. She is far more important as a symbol than she ever was as a person. She was one of the ordinary people of Fishguard who couldn't afford to run away like those who were wealthier. She had no choice but to stand and fight and by doing so she has passed into history.

The event was also remembered on its bicentennial in 1997 when the 100 foot long *Last Invasion Tapestry* was sewn by 78 volunteers. You can see this jolly piece of work today in the library. And the whole thing seems rather comical today. But it wasn't. Real people were frightened and real people died. The French when they landed appeared to have arrived to fight and to conquer. Why else would they come? And they appeared out of the sea in the night, fully armed and completely alien. It must have been a very frightening experience.

Today though, we remember it for the way women in traditional Welsh costume defeated the French and this reputation has its finest expression in Harri Webb's poem, *The Women of Fishguard*.

> *The Frenchmen took one look at them*
> *And in panic they did flee,*
> *Cried oo-la-la, and then ta-ta*
> *And jumped into the sea,*
> *And said to one another*
> *As back to France they swam*
> *We'd have stayed at home if we'd only known*
> *That we'd have to take on Mam.*

Flint, Flintshire
Catherine Dennis,
Buried in Linthwaite, Yorkshire 1891

The Linthwaite Murder

We parked the car, walked through the gate of Christ Church, looked to the left, found the grave and then departed. After all, this was Laithwaite just outside Huddersfield and we had no cause to linger. But we had done our duty; we had paid our respects to Catherine (Kate) Dennis, a forgotten 16-year-old Welsh servant girl from Flint, who was murdered here in the shadows of the Pennines in 1891.

It is a tragic story, of a life casually snatched away, and of a crime leaving terrible emotional wreckage in its wake, in both Linthwaite and Flint. For Catherine was not the only victim of that dreadful August day.

Catherine Dennis, so far from home

Her father Edward was a labourer at the Flint Chemical Works, and the family lived on Corporation Street. There were four daughters and the family had relocated here from Holyhead in Anglesey. Kate had last visited home in Flint for her holidays at Whitsuntide. She had gone into service when she was fourteen in the Ivy Green public house (known locally as The Ivy Hotel) on Manchester Road in Linthwaite. It was a long way from home, but perhaps she was in West Yorkshire because she had a cousin Edith, also in service, in nearby Slaithwaite.

In the year she had been there, Kate had shown herself to be invaluable. The landlady, Mrs Brook, knew she could rely upon her entirely. She was the best servant she ever had and so she left Kate in charge of the pub when she went off to do some shopping on a Friday afternoon in August 1891. There were only a handful of customers that lunchtime.

Later in the afternoon a butcher's boy from the Co-op arrived with a delivery. He found the pub empty, apart from Catherine, lying on her back with her arms stretched out on the landing at the top of the stairs. Her throat had been cut and there was a pool of blood under her head. It was clear that there had been a very violent struggle, for her wrists were badly bruised. Her clothes were disarranged. An attempt had been made to rape and strangle her before she was stabbed.

Local people rushed to the Ivy Green, handing over money to see the scene of the crime and Kate's body. '*Sympathy for the murdered girl seemed to be almost entirely forgotten,*' in the unexpected thrill of the moment.

Two men were immediately arrested but they were soon released. The police realised they should have been looking for James Stockwell. He had been in the pub that afternoon, eating pie in the kitchen using a thin-bladed knife as a fork. He had since disappeared. His wife hadn't seen him, but then they no longer lived together. But she confirmed that one of his casual occupations was as a pig killer.

Stockwell was on the run.

There were possible sightings of the fugitive. Was he that strange man in a wood? Or the man hiding behind a wall? Or the one seen leaning against a gate? An Irish vagrant was arrested in Dewsbury after confessing to the murder but he probably just fancied a night in the cells and was released the following morning.

There was considerable outrage at the crime. Kate had been a popular girl. *The Yorkshire Evening Post* spoke of customers who *'delighted in hearing her speak Welsh.'* She had *'everybody's good word.'* She had arrived in the north as *'petite'* and in the brisk Yorkshire air had grown into *'a fine strapping young woman.'* The people of Linthwaite were touched by the appearance in their town of Kate's parents who were entirely Welsh speaking and *'utterly weighed down with grief.'* They collected money to pay for her headstone. At the funeral, a wreath of white flowers was laid by members of the Linthwaite Brass Band and *The Huddersfield Chronicle* was moved to publish a poem in her memory. It ended with the verse

> *The base monster who has done*
>
> *Such cruel wrong to thee*
>
> *Shall be regarded as a blot*
>
> *On our humanity.*

I think you now understand why you haven't heard of this poem before.

There was no sign of Stockwell and people began to think that he might have thrown himself into a canal or a reservoir. But he hadn't. After seventeen days hiding on the moors, he broke into his mother's house in the early morning. When she found him there, emaciated and dirty, she asked him *'Oh dear me, lad, has tha' had anything to do with that lass?'* Stockwell told her that he was innocent and so Mrs Stockwell went to the police and told them where he was.

He gave himself up quietly. He was *'a wretched object…his clothes were in rags.'* In fact, he hadn't wandered far. He had hidden under nearby haystacks and in ditches and had eaten merely a handful of beans taken from a garden. He said that *'for three days he wept with remorse.'* Perhaps arrest came as a relief. It certainly prevented a probable lynching if he'd been found.

When he was in front of the magistrate, he pleaded guilty to the murder but when he appeared before Justice Wright at the West Riding Assizes in Leeds in December 1891, he changed his plea to *'not guilty.'*

Kate was described as *'truthful, honest and good,'* words which could never be used to describe Stockwell. He claimed that whilst he and Kate had never had a relationship, she had been teasing him by knocking off his hat and, *'in a moment of passion,'* he tried to get hold of her. She ran upstairs and then he couldn't remember what happened. He admitted to drinking heavily for two or three days before the murder and it was felt far more likely that, seriously drunk, he had fallen asleep. Kate had tried to wake him by tugging on his hair so that she could get on with her work. He had woken suddenly in such a wild and terrifying rage that she fled upstairs but there could be no escape. He attacked her and stabbed her, as he stabbed pigs, in the neck.

His only hope lay in the tragic catalogue of mental disorders that ran through his family which the defence lawyer presented in court. His mother had spent seven months in Wakefield Asylum some years before. He sister *'had been insane for four years at least,'* one uncle had committed suicide and another, who had been restrained by being roped down to his bed, had died in Wadsley Asylum, just like his grandmother.

The jury was unimpressed. They retired but returned quickly within ten minutes with a guilty verdict. Stockwell was condemned to death.

A petition was raised to obtain a pardon for him and sent to the Home Secretary on the basis that the *'terrible scourge of insanity,'* exacerbated by previous severe head injuries he had received, was the cause of his behaviour. But the petition was rejected and his execution was confirmed for 5 January 1892 at Armley Gaol in Leeds.

Then, just days before the execution, Kate's mother died in a Flintshire asylum. *'Soon after the murder she lost her reason, through the murder preying on her mind.'* Mrs Stockwell was taken into Wadsley Asylum at almost at the same time.

It was reported that James Stockwell walked firmly to the scaffold where death appeared to be almost instantaneous. Before he died, he wrote letters to his relatives containing warnings about the evils of drink. He also wrote, *I leave you with my most affectionate love to my dear mother. May God have mercy on her and if it be His will, return to her health and strength again.'*

His plea did not work. The poor woman, who had handed over her own son James to the police as a murderer, died in Wadsley Asylum two months after his execution.

You can go to Linthwaite of course. I won't stand in your way. It lies on the A62 between Huddersfield and Oldham. Over the Pennines in Lancashire, the road edges past Saddleworth Moor. It is not a nice place. I will understand if you don't fancy going there.

Glynneath, Neath Port Talbot

William Jones, 1917
Buried in Locre Hospice Cemetery, France

Shot at Dawn

We went to the battlefields of the Ypres Salient to find William Jones, one man amongst thousands. You can go there and be overwhelmed by the number of casualties of World War One. There are graves everywhere around Ypres and every white gravestone that shines in the sun represents a life not fully lived. It is a vast sea of unfulfilled potential and hopes, every stone a story.

There are huge cemeteries, like Tyne Cot for example with over 11,800 graves, some of which contain two or three unidentified comrades. The Menin Gate Memorial in Ypres itself remembers 54,900 soldiers whose bodies disappeared completely, turned to dust by the guns. There wasn't enough space for the rest of them, so the wall at the rear of Tyne Cot has another 34,800 names engraved upon it. The scale is staggering. So why should I look for one particular grave amongst so many? William is no relative of mine, he won no medals, he was, as far as I know, no one's father. Just another young soldier, still a boy, a casualty of war.

Private William Jones, a seventeen-year-old Welsh-speaking boy from Glynneath, with probably a tenuous grasp of English, a volunteer in the Royal Welsh Fusiliers, was condemned to death for desertion and executed by his comrades on 25 October 1917. William Jones was shot at dawn.

Locre Hospice Cemetery

There are only a modest 238 graves in Locre Hospice Cemetery where William lies, on the border between Belgium and France. You can find it in the village, which is called either Locre or Loker, depending on which side of the border you are on. We had to park some distance away and walk down between houses to a small corner of a field. Finding William was easy. He is in the middle of a neat row against the wall, behind which the neighbouring field was, appropriately, muddy and lifeless. It was finding out about him that was more difficult.

The restricted range of surnames in Wales is not always a help during research. William Jones is not a unique name in Wales – perhaps you reading this now, or your father, is called William Jones - and so it is hard to establish the facts about him. He was probably about seventeen when he deserted and since he was said to have been in the army for two years, it indicates that he enlisted when he was still fifteen. The newspapers report that thirty young men enlisted in Glynneath in January 1915. Was he one of them?

He could have visited Mr. P Sheppard who was appointed the village recruiting agent in April that year or he might have strolled along to see Mr Phillips in the Lamb and Flag who was on the committee. The Recruiting Officer in Neath turned a circus wagon into a recruiting office, adorned with posters proclaiming *Come inside and join the Army. The cheapest show in the Fair.* Perhaps he went there. But wherever he did it, William became a private in the Royal Welsh Fusiliers and served as a stretcher bearer. You ask yourself, was he really old enough to do such an awful job? There could be no hiding from the terrible reality of death and dismemberment when you are struggling to carry bodies away to dressing stations. It would be no surprise at all if he found his duties profoundly disturbing. Any one of us could have cracked under that sort of strain.

His commanding officer said he was a good soldier, but War Office records suggest that by 1917 he was serving under a suspended sentence of death following desertion. In such circumstances going missing for a second time was a very dangerous thing to do.

William disappeared on 15 June 1917 after taking a wounded soldier to a dressing station and the army lost track of him completely. In fact he showed remarkable resourcefulness - he was one of only eight soldiers who managed to desert and successfully cross the Channel - and made his way home to Glynneath. His name could have offered him anonymity in Wales. How could the army ever distinguish one William Jones from another? The Commonwealth War Graves Commission records that 217 soldiers called William Jones died in 1917. In fact during the course of the war, 726 William Joneses serving in the British Army were killed, along with sixty-two at sea and five airmen. The numbers are astonishing. However, anonymity is rarely available in a Welsh village.

In addition, William might have come home but he'd brought the war with him. There was no escape from it. In July there was a concert at the Church Institute when money was distributed to *the 'dependents of fallen Heroes and discharged soldiers ...by the Glynneath Male Voice Choir.'* Sick and wounded soldiers in the Neath and District War Hospital at Penrhiewtyn were entertained with a variety show *('including the National Anthems of the Allies')* by the Wesley Church. In August, a convoy of another 120 wounded soldiers arrived there from the Front and in September, a further 300 of them were brought to Glynneath. They were greeted by the local drum and fife band and prizes were awarded for the best fancy costume and elocution.

Lance Corporal Clifford Protheroe, home on leave in August, was presented with a nice wallet and valuable contents by the Glyn Neath Billiard Club. On 1 September 1917 the *Aberdare Leader* under the headline, *Glynneath Heroes,* reported that Gunner Rowland and Private Hall had been killed in action. *'Glynneath would be poorer for the loss of these promising young men.'*

Perhaps William began to realise that he would never be welcomed home as a hero or mourned. Only if he were wounded would he ever be entertained so lavishly. As a deserter, there would never be an honourable mention for him in the paper. All this is entirely speculative, but what is certain is that in September, he handed himself in at the police station in Neath and he was returned to the army in Bristol. I hope that I am wrong, but I wonder sometimes whether his mother persuaded him to do so, believing that because he was young, he would be forgiven. If this was the case then what a burden she would have carried. William told them that he had been wounded and had been evacuated home – a ridiculous claim that was quickly dismantled.

He was returned to his regiment at Ypres. There was a court martial, based upon a presumption of guilt. It led to an inevitable verdict, with no appeals procedure. Once the sentence was ratified, the execution proceeded mercifully quickly. Private 15954 William

Jones was shot on Kemmel Hill on 25 October 1917 by members of his own battalion. Like all condemned men, William Jones would have been tied and blindfolded, with a white target pinned to his heart. The officer would ensure the soldier was dead, administering a shot to the head if necessary, and then the body quickly buried.

The firing squad would often be immediately sent on leave.

William Jones, a boy.

William is not the only soldier in Locre Hospice who was executed for desertion. Private Denis Blakemore from Shrewsbury had also been previously condemned to death for desertion and the sentence suspended. Like William's, a further offence could not be forgiven. He ran away prior to an assault at Messines and was picked up after eighteen days on the run in Boulogne. Unlike William, he didn't make it across the Channel. There is nothing on either grave to show that they were executed. Indeed, some parents never knew what happened to their sons in these circumstances. Perhaps neither mother was ever told anything, other than their son had died of wounds.

Eventually William Jones' name was engraved on the Glynneath War Memorial following the pardon issued to the soldiers executed in the First World War in 2006. There is still no acknowledgement there of his fate. You must go to the National Arboretum in Lichfield for that.

William was a victim of the war just as much as anyone else. Sadly, he was not the only man serving with a Welsh regiment to be executed. Most were privates and most were found guilty of desertion, the inevitable consequence of the horror of the trenches. There were fifteen of them, though they were not all born in Wales. One Welsh soldier, Jesse Short from Nantyglo, served with the Northumberland Fusiliers and was the only man shot for his part in a serious mutiny at a camp in Etaples in September 1917.

I have always had particular sympathy for Private William Scholes, who was another under a suspended death sentence for desertion. He was serving with the South Wales Borderers and kept going absent because he felt the allowance given to his widowed mother, for whom he was the sole support, was measly. A principled stand certainly, but perhaps in the circumstances not wise. He was executed in August 1918 and buried in the Borre Cemetery in Northern France. Running away might be the best way to escape danger, as the Chinese proverb would have it, but in the army it was understandably a crime. Today we see things differently.

Murder of course is something different and two others from that unhappy group of fifteen, William Price and Richard Morgan of the Welsh Regiment, were executed for shooting Company Sergeant Major Hayes on 20 January 1915 near Bethune in France (the same day incidentally that the regimental goat died of a heart attack in the snow.) In *Goodbye to All That* the author Robert Graves maintained it was all a terrible mistake. They had been trying to shoot their platoon sergeant.

Gresford, Wrexham
The Gresford Mining Disaster, 1934

They died for nine shillings a day

Accidents and death were always a part of the miner's lot, for life has always been fragile underground. At some point most miners accompanied the dead body of a colleague, taken home after a rock fall. But the Gresford Mining disaster in September 1934 was different. It was a consequence of neglect. It was not just an accident waiting to happen. Every day the miners expected an explosion. The only thing they couldn't know was whether they would be working when it happened. When it did, 261 men never went home.

The names of the miners who died through neglect

Gresford Colliery, just outside Wrexham, was owned by United Westminster and Wrexham Colliers. There were two shafts about 50 yards apart. One was the Martin and the other was the Dennis, named after the pit owners. The Dennis shaft was 690 metres deep and from the bottom of the shaft there was a long journey to the coal faces themselves. The mine was the most significant employer in the area, employing over 2,000 men, from most of the local villages. But the colliery was at risk. It was operating at a loss and the pressure was on from the owners to make a profit. Managers were desperately trying to maintain output, whilst at the same time refusing to invest in the infrastructure.

From our perspective, there appears to have been an air of desperation about the mine. There was inadequate management and at the same time the spectre of unemployment hung over the miners themselves. They had to turn a blind eye to the conditions in which they worked because there was no alternative employment. The workers at Gresford were not unionised because they could not afford the fees and in the circumstances, no one dared risk being labelled as a troublemaker. Working conditions were awful. Ventilation was inadequate and it was uncomfortably hot. Men worked in shorts, with holes drilled through their clogs to allow the sweat to escape. They were surrounded by coal dust and gas. Miners would often go home in a gas-induced daze. There were numerous breaches of regulations relating to the firing of explosives to release coal from the face. There was no firefighting equipment and no available water. And outside the mine there were no jobs. The place was inefficient, desperate and unsafe.

Saturday 22 September 1934, at 2.08 am, the Dennis Section was destroyed by an explosion. Six men came out. 261 were left behind. At the time the shift was over-manned. There should have been 195 on the night shift. There was a football match later that day between Tranmere and Wrexham and some men were working a double shift so that they could go and see it.

People rushed to the mine. Rescue teams were organised but immediately shortcomings were noted. There was no map of the workings available to guide them and no clear idea of how many people were working. In fact, it took them over 24 hours to confirm the number of men missing.

Three men of the first rescue team died when they were overcome by gas. As soon as they descended to the bottom of the shaft, their canary fell dead in its cage. They panicked, their nose clips came off and the carbon monoxide got them. Only their leader, John Williams, kept his head and survived.

It was soon obvious that any further rescue attempts were futile. It was not possible to penetrate any distance into the workings. It was clear that nothing could have survived the fire and the gas. Serious explosions continued deep within the mine throughout Sunday and by the evening the decision was taken to seal the pit, to extinguish the flames by excluding oxygen. Only eleven bodies were ever recovered.

The final death in this terrible story occurred when the seal blew off and killed George Brown, a rescue worker on the surface.

The disaster provoked a huge response across the country. Poor people sent whatever they could. The disaster Relief fund records hundreds of small donations, sometimes as small as 6d, from those who had nothing much themselves. A fishmonger sent 200 boxes of kippers. A farmer in Kent sent three tons of apples. The Northampton Town Boot Manufacturers offered to replace any boots belonging to the rescue team that were damaged in the fires. Childless couples offered to adopt fatherless children. Widowers sent letters looking for widows to act as housekeepers, with a view to marriage. And all the while the mine owners did their best to protect themselves. It is believed that they destroyed evidence that showed their lack of vigilance, of checks not carried out, of reports falsified.

Recovery teams re-entered the sealed pit in 1935 in response to the official inquiry; however, the company allowed only its own officials to enter the Dennis section because of what they called the dangerous conditions, and the miners' bodies were soon sealed forever. It was believed by many that this was merely to hide any evidence of management neglect, since none of the theories offered about the causes of the explosion could never now be proved.

The miners' legal representative, Sir Stafford Cripps, made a strong case that the explosion had been triggered by the use of explosives in an area where gas had accumulated. The management claimed that ignition had occurred from a spark from a telephone used to warn miners of the appearance of gas. In this way, they tried to deny that poor working practices were to blame. But even that didn't convince. The telephones were not safe, since they hadn't been enclosed in flameproof cases. In fact, the miners themselves were accused by the managers of being responsible for the unsafe conditions in the mine because they had not complained. How could they and still keep their jobs?

The enquiry found that the colliery management, the firemen and the inspectors had not performed their duties properly. It was suspected that shot firing had triggered the explosion. Nevertheless, the exact location of the initial explosion could not be identified and there was no finding of criminal negligence.

And in that revealing and long-standing tradition the dead miners had their pay docked for not completing their shift.

Gresford colliery reopened six months after the disaster. Families continued to grieve, denied the closure that a proper funeral could bring. When the mines were nationalized in 1947, almost all the operating records relating to Gresford Colliery were destroyed. It was eventually closed on economic grounds in November 1973.

One of the great folk songs – *The Gresford Disaster*, most

memorably recorded by the Albion Band -captures the essence of the tragedy and tells the story much better than I can. In simple words, written allegedly by John Williams, the only survivor of the first rescue team, the causes and the consequences of the explosion in the Colliery are outlined. You don't really need anything else. You can listen to it on YouTube. Using the hymn tune *How Sweet the Name of Jesus Sounds,* the Albion Band tell you everything you need to know, the raw power of the music reflecting perfectly the horror and anger that washes over you when you consider what happened.

> *Down there in the dark they are lying*
>
> *They died for nine shillings a day.*
>
> *They have worked out their shift and now they must lie*
>
> *In the darkness until Judgement Day.*

There is a large open space there now. An industrial estate, a playing field. And a community with a generation of its men still entombed beneath our feet.

The pit head wheel at Gresford

Gresford is still a name that resounds through social history. The only hint of what once was there is in the pit head wheel and the names that this memorial carries. It lies just off the A183 Chester – Wrexham bypass. There is a power and a truth in its simplicity. And yet much of the world passes by without a glance.

This is where exploitation and the naked pursuit of money lead. It is best that we don't forget. Gresford is there to tell us that it should never be allowed to happen again, anywhere.

Hafod, Ceredigion
Thomas Johnes, 1816

The Hafod Estate

Thomas Johnes had a mad idea; that you could tame and order a landscape as wild and extensive as the Ystwyth Valley.

The stone on the family vault outside Eglwys Newydd

Like others, he believed that human intervention could improve what nature had created.

But the Hafod Estate, no matter how beautiful, was always a wild and unsustainable dream.

You can find the estate on the B4574 in Ceredigion as it leads away from Devil's Bridge. It was once owned by the monks of Strata Florida, but with the dissolution of the monasteries, it passed into the ownership of the Herbert family, who were interested in exploiting the timber and the mineral resources.

Thomas Johnes was born in Ludlow in 1748 and educated, first at Eton, and then at the University of Edinburgh. He became an MP and took a military commission. But his life changed on a visit to the family property at Hafod which he had inherited. He was captivated by the estate. He wrote to a friend to tell him that he had found paradise and Hafod became a passion that never left him.

His first wife Maria died in 1782 within a year of their marriage. He then married his cousin, Jane Johnes, in the face of considerable family disapproval. Together they took up residence at Hafod and in 1784 their only child, Mariamne, was born.

They built a mansion designed by Thomas Baldwin of Bath and finished in 1788. It was built in Bath stone, which glows in the gentler climate along the Avon but the soft stone was not a wise choice for driving Welsh rain. It weathered quickly.

In 1793 he employed the architect, John Nash, to add a library and a conservatory. It was a grand building, sheltering in its green valley, and was painted by Turner, one the many famous figures who was drawn to the estate. Coleridge is said to have based the 'pleasure domes' of Xanadu in his poem *Kubla Khan* upon the shape of the Hafod building. The house was regarded as *'one of the most attractive and admired seats in the principality'* and was noted for its library. It contained a printing press and produced literary texts, particularly of French Chronicles from the Middle Ages, about which Johnes, a noted translator, was something of an expert. Every effort was made to create a cultured environment that reflected the very best of human achievement.

Johnes was clearly a benevolent man and devoted his energies to the estate and its people.

He built cottages, employed doctors and started a school for girls. His influence was everywhere. Over a period of five years, over 2 million trees were planted. He certainly brought employment to the area, as he tried to carve something out of the wilderness.

The estate was designed to be enjoyed on foot, providing an enormous variety of experiences. His intention was to provide sketching stations where the privileged could stop and sketch the views that lay before them,

His visitors stayed either at Hafod itself or in the Hafod Arms at Devil's Bridge, which was built for the purpose. From there they would travel up to the estate to look at the interior of the house, the kitchen garden and then they would follow the paths until it was time to go home, admiring '*majestic mountains and romantic rocky precipices, rivers foaming in cataracts.*'

Yet the whole project was dogged by fire, destruction and tragedy.

Whilst Thomas was away in London, the house was destroyed in a fire in 1807 which '*broke out early in the morning; and, with the exception of a very small portion of the books, rescued from the flames by the intrepidity of Mrs. Johnes, the whole of the library, consisting of many thousand volumes, several of the paintings, and nearly all the splendid furniture of the house, were consumed.*' Jane and Mariamne then watched the destruction of their home from a hill on the estate. What an awful sight it must have been, with the fames lighting up the vast darkness of the valley.

The house was re-built by Baldwin again, at great expense, but the drain upon the estate was immense and it was funded largely by the sale of timber. However, the greatest tragedy of all was Mariamne.

She was very intelligent and she had a great interest in the natural world. She was educated by tutors, who taught her music, drawing and languages but it was botany that was her greatest love and from an early age she corresponded with the leading naturalists of her time.

But there was a problem. When she was ten, she became chronically sick. There have been a number of subsequent diagnoses, which have included tuberculosis and congenital syphilis. Certainly she was very ill. She suffered from tumours and curvature of the spine and required a steel brace to support her. She never married and died suddenly in 1811, aged 27, on a visit to London.

An arch fit for a king

And in some ways Johnes' purpose disappeared with her. In 1810 everything was possible. He built an arch over the road at the highest part of the estate to mark the golden Jubilee of King George. Then her death tore the heart out of the family and all the energy that had maintained the estate suddenly dissipated. It was too great a task and the money was running out.

In 1815 the Johnes moved to Dawlish and Thomas died a year later in April 1816. Paradise had made him bankrupt. It absorbed his time, his energy, his money. And it destroyed him.

It was sold for £70,000 to the Duke of Newcastle in 1833. He was a highly unpopular owner but he made one significant contribution to the sad history of Hafod. The Johnes family had commissioned a statue of their beloved Mariamne from the great Victorian sculptor Francis Chantry. But Johnes was unable to pay for it and it remained in London until the Duke settled the bill and moved it to Eglwys Newydd on the estate.

The beautiful Eglwys Newydd

Johnes had replaced the original church on the estate in 1801, with something far more elegant, designed by James Wyatt who had restored Salisbury Cathedral. Behind the church there are the railings which surround the Johnes family vault. Within it lie the

110

remains of Thomas, Jane and Mariamne, absorbed into the soil to which they devoted their lives.

Chantry's sculpture within the church brought many to see it and yet this too was hunted down by tragedy. In April 1932 the church, which had just had a new heating system, caught fire. The nearest telephone was at Devil's Bridge and by the time the Fire Brigade arrived from Aberystwyth, the roof has already fallen in. Their jets of water cracked the overheated marble of the statue. It shattered into fragments.

It is still there, a suitable symbol for the failed project that the Hafod estate became. A thing of beauty that time has taken away from us. It is the final tragedy of the Johnes family. The vicar told me it would cost too much to have it properly restored or replicated, so it still sits there, forlornly speaking of sorrow, rather than beauty.

The estate was owned by a succession of timber merchants. But it seemed to need more money than it could generate. Where once it was the most visited place in Wales, it became lost and forgotten and by 1946 it was declared derelict. In 1958 what remained of the mansion was demolished by explosives as a health and safety measure.

The ruins are still there. You can scramble over them. I have. You can see features appearing through the rubble – a brick arch, a cornice.

The Hafod Estate Trust is now helping the estate to re- emerge from beneath the tangled embrace of the rhododendrons and the undergrowth. You can take fantastic walks through the estate, with different levels of difficulty. (The Gentleman's Walk. The Ladies Walk) The walks are now tamed and clearly marked, but they remain wild and isolated. You can find yourself down the river and suddenly think you are in Alaska.

Mariamne's garden is slowly emerging too. We know now that

the garden paths were originally made from crushed quartz, which would have sparkled so much in the sunshine. Another thing that we have lost.

Landshipping, Pembrokeshire
Joseph Harts, 1844

The Garden Pit Disaster

Landshipping is an unassuming little hamlet with an unusual name, between Haverfordwest and Tenby, where a quiet narrow road eventually decides to wander alongside the peaceful estuary. Here in a layby at the old quayside, with beautiful views across the water, you will find a modest but poignant memorial to forty dead miners.

If mining is Pembrokeshire's lost industry, then the Garden Pit catastrophe in Landshipping in 1844 is its forgotten disaster.

A terrible story from such a beautiful place

Coal mining went on in Pembrokeshire for centuries and by 1700 coal was the area's major export. It was high quality anthracite, too. The coal-bearing rocks stretched in a narrow strip from Carmarthen Bay to St Brides Bay in the west. The mines might have been small but they were productive and profitable.

Mine owners followed the seam, always, no matter where it went. After all, their wealth was based entirely on the coal and consequently mines went beneath the sea. Garden Pit in Landshipping, Pembrokeshire opened in 1788 and soon the shaft was 67ft deep and extended out under the eastern branch of the Cleddau River. Not surprisingly, the pit was known as a particularly wet one, but it was an important operation for the owner, Colonel Sir Hugh Owen, producing 10,000 tons per year, which was taken away by sea from the purpose-built quay. It was the same reason why the more familiar Saundersfoot was developed – for the transportation of coal.

But the workings around Landshipping were not deep. It was said that the workers could hear the sound of oars in boats in the estuary above them. They were working only three feet below the bed of a powerful tidal river. Conditions, of course, were dreadful. Ventilation was especially poor, but then how could it be otherwise, with all that water above?

The Coal Mines Regulation Act had been passed by parliament in 1842 and made it illegal for women, and children under ten years of age, to work underground. The law however was widely ignored. It was enforced by just one inspector who covered the whole of Britain and he was required to give prior notice of a visit anyway. And Pembrokeshire was a long way from anywhere.

The Garden Pit had a chequered history, for it had never been very safe. There had been, for example, an explosion in 1830 which killed five young miners. But death doesn't only come from fire; water can be just as deadly.

The part of the mine which was being worked in February 1844

114

hadn't been used for a while following a significant leak of salt water through the roof. However, after it had been closed for three years, someone decided that it was safe to open up the tunnel again. On the afternoon of 14 February 1844, there were 58 miners working on the shift, hacking out coal and dragging it back to the pit shaft. They were not the happiest group of workers. They were concerned by the entry of water and left the mine, refusing to work because it was too dangerous. Their instincts were dismissed, they were re-assured and sent back underground.

The first sign of trouble came at about 4pm when a tremendous rush of wind suddenly shot up the shaft, involuntarily forcing the hands and arms of those working at the surface high into the air. Down below, men were blown off their feet and all lights were extinguished as the air was pushed out, for water had broken in with terrible violence. On the river itself a series of violent eddies, like whirlpools, formed in the cold winter water close to shore, as it forced its way into the pit.

A small group of miners gathered at the bottom of the shaft, pleading for help. Young boys were desperately trying to climb up the pit shaft. Horses were used to haul four men and fourteen boys up to safety in the landing tub normally used for the coal. Nobody else managed to get out. When they dropped it again, it came back containing nothing but water.

It had happened so quickly. Forty miners were lost, over thirty of them trapped at the far end of the workings. The survivors saw that '*a portion of the ground underneath the mud on the side of the river, a little above the low water mark, had given way and the tide rushed into the fissure so as to drown the works.*' Those working on the wrong side of the fissure, further out at the far end of the level, did not have a hope.

Men descended the shaft and plumbed the water with grappling hooks but found nothing. The *Carmarthen Journal* said that the inundation '*took place with the suddenness of a dream, a few moments of horror and all was over.'*

There was a reminder of the disaster the following day when an explosion happened in the middle of the river, caused by the pressure of water on air trapped deep within the mine. Large pieces of timber were thrown into the air as the ground expelled these remnants from the broken pit.

What indeed was the price of coal? Disaster, distress and destitution, for all the local mine workings were ultimately interconnected and all were flooded, representing a terrible loss of employment. In moments such as these, lives had been cruelly ended and other lives changed forever.

Concerts were held to raise money for the families and contributions were sent to the *Pembroke Herald* to aid *'those poor creatures who, by a calamity of so dreadful a character, are thus unavoidably thrown on the sympathy of the public…sad indeed the condition of those who, by such a stroke, are at once deprived of everything.'* The Queen sent £20 to the fund and, though other contributions were by necessity much more modest, by April the amount raised was in excess of £364, the equivalent of over £20,000 today.

I have to report that not only have the records of the inquest been lost, but also, I have been unable to find any reports of any inquest or enquiry in the contemporary press. Those lost were just ordinary people, barely leaving less than a thumbprint on history and therefore, perhaps, expendable. There was no reason for a fuss; these things happen, after all. Mining was a dangerous occupation, everyone knew that. The manager of the Garden Pit who sent the miners back to work was exonerated.

However, things did not go so well for the owner Sir Hugh Owen. The loss of the mine provoked a financial crisis in the Owen family. Ty Mawr, their Big House at the heart of the estate is still visible, but the land at Landshipping was eventually sold to the Stanley family.

This was a terrible disaster that had a huge impact on a small distant community. You will see this when you examine the details on the memorial stone. It was first erected by the villagers in 2002 and then in 2019 a new memorial was rededicated with an updated plaque. It is clear that many of the dead were related to each other. Some surnames occur more than once, like Cole and Llewellin. Joseph Picton died with three of his sons, leaving behind a widow and five other children. James Davies died with one son, leaving a widow and five children.

The original memorial listed seven names where the first was given only as 'Miner'. These are believed to have been women and children, employed and killed in the pit that day in spite of the legislation; observance of the law did not seem to stretch as far as Pembrokeshire. Other names give ages as low as nine or 11. In one case a person was listed simply as "child". Research now suggests that this was almost certainly Joseph Harts. He was four years old.

The Garden Pit disaster was reported right across the country, from Westmoreland to London, from Cork to Essex, from Bristol to Dundee, with words like *'dreadful,'* *'awful,'* *'terrible,'* *destructive,'* *'fatal,'* *'melancholy,'* *'catastrophe.'* But no one seems to have felt the need to question the illegality of working practises.

In 1906, the press reported that one of three sisters who lived in a small cottage in Landshipping, Elizabeth Butland, had worked in the Garden Pit sixty-two years earlier, for the going rate of 4½d a day. A man was paid 1 shilling. Two of her brothers were killed in the disaster, trapped in a collapsing tunnel beneath a river, and you can see their names on the memorial stone – John, 17 and Thomas, 10.

It is such a humbling detail.

Llandegfan, Anglesey
James Hannett, 1878

Tuckey, Parkin, Dixon, Crewe

You can find Eglwys St Tegfan in Llandegfan in Anglesey. It is a pretty place which looks down on the Menai Straight and across to the mainland. It is peaceful and well-tended, reflecting the history of a hardworking rural community. But there is something unusual in the churchyard. Look carefully and you will find a collection of five very distinctive headstones. When we were there, a flush of snowdrops had gathered in front of one of the stones like a tribute. It is the least these gravestones deserve.

Tuckey, Parkin, Dixon, Crewe

They each have an anchor and a chain design and carry the name of a ship, *The Clio*. The inscription at the top of the stone is from Proverbs and reads *Those that seek me early shall find me*. Are these reassuring words? Or are they chilling? Because when you examine them, you can see that the headstones all are inscribed with the names of young boys.

These stones and these names bring together Anglesey and Montevideo on the same piece of grey local slate, in sad and moving stories. For these are the graves of boys from the Industrial Training Vessel, *The Clio*.

What strikes you immediately is the extent of the loss. You will find the names of 29 boys on 5 different headstones which stand lost and neglected, like the boys themselves. The headstones stand now at angles, as if battling against the ocean swell in this beautiful and peaceful cemetery, fighting against the relentless incursion of the long grass.

The Clio was a floating workhouse or orphanage which was moored in the Menai Straight from 1877 to May 1919 and these gravestones remember the boys who died either on board, or at sea later. Their names feature as lists, like a bureaucratic exercise. Indeed, eleven boys are mentioned on both sides of one stone as if to save space and to cut costs. It is a tragic register from a floating school.

In fact, such industrial training ships prefigured the concept of vocational training that some people today find quite enticing. But there was a sense of finality about it all. Someone else was making your decisions for you. They told you that this is your life. That a path has been marked out for you that you must follow. That your expectations and your horizons have been chosen for you by someone else.

Obviously, those involved felt they were doing good work. Given their paternalistic view of the world, they never seemed to consider it otherwise. The idea was to help the poor find jobs and in so doing to remove boys from the workhouse. The boys were given training in naval life, acquiring the skills and discipline allegedly required for teenage boys and also to provide a reservoir of recruits. It was a production line responding to supply and demand, a simple way of plugging the skills gap. As the supervisory board said, do your work well and *'worldly success is assured.'* An element of extended support was offered, too. A home was provided in Liverpool to which they could return between voyages after they had left *The Clio*.

But it was a dangerous world. Boys died frequently. There is a report in the Caernarfon and Denbigh Herald for 24 August 1878. *'A young lad named Hallett was amusing himself by exercising on the yard arm'* when he fell to the deck. He died 2 days later.

The inquest was held at what is today The Gazelle Inn on the Anglesey side of the Garth ferry. It didn't take long to find a verdict of Accidental Death, though the coroner did advise the staff *'to place nets under the yards whilst the boys were being exercised upon them, the deceased having fallen 60 or 70 feet to the deck.'* We are told that *'120 boys attended his funeral in charge of Mr. Delaney, the Chief Officer. His coffin was covered in the Union Jack.'*

Of course, we notice that the reporter manages to spell his name incorrectly and gives the impression that his Christian name is not important. There is no boy named Hallett in the graveyard.

At least we know his proper name. He was James Hannett and he received more respect in his death that he ever did alive. He was eleven years old and had been on board for five weeks when he died. He was from Manchester. His father was dead and his mother in prison for an assault, which he is why he was there. What else could be done with him?

In death he shares his gravestone with John Healey, who also fell from the rigging on 29 June 1880. He was 15. Those nets recommended by the coroner do not appear to have been effective.

James Hannett. 11 Years old

The training ship functioned as an orphanage, as a place to park abandoned and difficult boys and give them training for a future life at sea. Indeed they were described as "*scholars training for the sea.*" They were from disadvantaged backgrounds or they had already been in trouble. They were generally young and undernourished. The Census register for 1881 carries details of their birthplace. They come from all over the country – including William Hodgkins born on a barge.

Bullying was not uncommon in such an environment. One boy, William Crook had been assaulted by older boys resulting in fatal head injuries in January 1905. Poor William. His name appears with ten others on a small stone sinking into the long grass and the soft earth. It is a small headstone but also a double-sided one, necessary to fit on all the names.

It was a harsh regime with limited food and accommodation. The boys slept in hammocks which could be very cold. All boots and clothes were made on-board. But it seems a desperate and dangerous place. Even those who survived and graduated to employment were not always any safer. Their work could take them across the world and some of the boys in Llandegfan died exotically, like John Parkin who was lost at sea with all hands, or Charles Dixon washed overboard off New Jersey or James Mort drowned off Montevideo. Most of them died however in accidents on board an old decaying vessel moored off Anglesey and trapped in the tides. Death appears to have been a part of the curriculum.

Life aboard was cramped and brutal and it is hardly surprising that the boys would run like monkeys through the rigging when they could. A taste of freedom, but a dangerous one.

The ship was regarded as a local curiosity. It became a tourist attraction in the same way that Bethlem Hospital did in London. It was a chance to see the poor and to feel that the exciting modern age in which you lived did its very best for those less fortunate than yourself. Training ships were always short of money and collected additional donations by taking visitors on board for a tour. Visitors could *Signal the ship from the Pier, for a well manned boat to convey them there and back for a trifling fee.*

Of course, it wasn't so good that you would choose to go there yourself. Far from it. Local parents used it as a threat. The children of Anglesey called it *the naughty children's ship.* To others it was a curiosity, an interesting tourist diversion, a floating borstal.

One visitor, Benjamin Goodfellow, went to visit, well provisioned with Cockles Antibilious Pills to combat the swell. In his journal he comments

what a fine thing it was to have put so many lads who would otherwise have been lost in evil in the way of earning an honest living for themselves, for on leaving the ship they can get situations with wages of about £2 per month.

And in some ways the solution to a social problem seems very enticing. It appeared to provide an escape route from poverty, a genuine career pathway. But a training ship could be a brutal place, preparing them for a job in which death was commonplace

These stones tell a sad and neglected story. There were a

number of ships around the coast. There was *The Akbar* on Merseyside and *The Cornwall* at Purfleet. Some training ships were established for prospective Merchant Navy officers. But the ships became unseaworthy and the demand for boys declined as crews became smaller.

The Clio, built as a 22-gun corvette at Sheerness in 1858, was broken up on Bangor beach in 1920.

All that remains now are those five graves in the churchyard, silent witnesses to incomplete and unfulfilled lives. We should not forget the boys or the unhappy stories which brought them to a decaying ship moored in the Menai Strait.

Llanelli, Carmarthenshire
Leonard Worsell and John H. John, 1911

The Llanelli Riot of 1911

The graves that symbolise this moment of shame stand clean and bright. They are a mute but a chilling reminder of one of the darkest moments in Britain's social history. The gravestones announce – 'Workers of the World Unite' and 'Fatally Shot by the Military.' Simple words which tell of a moment everyone did their best to forget. We are in the Box Cemetery and these are the graves of Leonard Worsell and John H. John, victims of the Llanelli Riot of August 1911.

The National Railway Strike of 1911 was prompted by serious grievances about pay. Average wages on the Railway were £1 a week – 20% below those of skilled workers elsewhere. In an act of solidarity, railwaymen were supported by miners and tinplate workers who received much better rates of pay themselves. One of these was John 'Jac' John, 21 years old, who was a millworker at the Morewood Tinplate works. Like all young men who have ever lived in Llanelli, he was described as a promising rugby player.

The dispute began on Thursday – and by the early hours of Friday Thomas Jones, a local Councillor, Magistrate and grocer, requested assistance from the army to maintain order in the town. The Home Secretary, Winston Churchill agreed. Anxiety, after all, was rife. The government feared that the country was heading towards revolution and the most important duty it had was to maintain order in the face of industrial unrest, and indeed anything else, which might threaten social order.

The Lancashire Fusiliers were sent down from Cardiff. They

had been stationed there after policing the Miner's Strike in Tonypandy. They were skilled and experienced and relations between the strikers and the troops on Friday were fine.

However, Thomas Jones did not want the strike sensitively policed. He wanted the strike broken – perhaps because as a shareholder in the Great Western Railway he was concerned about his dividends. More troops were ordered in – this time the Worcestershire Regiment under the command of Major Brownlow-Stuart. By now there were 370 soldiers in the town - which was hardly likely to calm the atmosphere in which the dispute was taking place.

On Saturday 19 August there was a mass picket at Llanelli Railway Station. This was a powerful gesture by the strikers, showing they could block the Great Western Railway. Sadly, what the railway workers saw as a negotiating strength, became a fatal weakness, since disruption to supply routes to troops in Ireland dealing with the Troubles there, could not be tolerated.

A train, allegedly carrying strike-breaking workers, tried to pass along the line through the town –enough to inflame further highly-charged emotions. The train had been held up and the Commanding Officer of the Worcesters ordered the troops to use bayonets to part the crowd. This allowed the train to creep through carefully, but strikers forced themselves on board and raked out the engine fire, thus immobilising the train. The troops who had followed it were trapped in a cutting, where the strikers threw stones at them. Major Brownlow-Stuart asked the JP to read the Riot Act, which he did, but so quietly and nervously that it is unlikely that anyone heard him.

It was the last time it was read in mainland Britain – and had fatal consequences. The major then ordered his men to fire their rifles. Shouts went out from the crowd that they should not worry. The shots would be blanks. But they were not. The rifles were loaded with live ammunition. Two men, one entirely unconnected

125

with the disturbance were shot – John 'Jac' John and Leonard Worsell. In that moment they became working class martyrs.

John H. John. Shot by the Military *Leonard Worsell. Shot by the Military*

Leonard was not a Llanelli man at all. He was 19 and came from Penge in South London and was visiting the Allt y Mynydd sanatorium near Llanybydder where he was convalescing after contracting TB. He had been shaving and had come into the garden of 6 High Street to see what all the fuss was about. After all strikers, including Jac John, had spilled into the garden. He stood there bare-chested, and in bare feet, watching the show.

Major Brownlow-Stuart said they were merely warning shots that unfortunately went astray; Major Brownlow-Stuart said that Leonard had bared his chest as an act of defiance, which naturally required a response. Some witnesses however, later claimed the two men were deliberately targeted. What is beyond dispute is that Leonard was shot through the heart. Jac received a serious and fatal chest wound. Others were wounded.

There was an inevitable explosion of rage. The Worcesters were forced to withdraw to the station and they barricaded themselves inside to shelter from the howling mob outside. Llanelli was poised on the very edge of an insurrection.

Shops were attacked and looted, starting inevitably with Thomas Jones' shop and the two of his farms outside town.

One man used dynamite to open an armoured freight truck,

looking for whatever he could get. Sadly the truck contained munitions and he was killed, along with three others, in a huge explosion. A soldier, Harold Spiers, refused to fire on the crowd. He was arrested but escaped and went on the run. There was a real fear that there might be a mutiny.

The streets were eventually cleared by another 300 soldiers from the Sussex Regiment who were rushed to the town. There were now almost 700 troops in Llanelli – an ordinary Welsh town had an army of occupation. In these circumstances, people with bayonet and baton wounds refused to seek treatment for fear of arrest. When Monday came the children at Bigyn School in the town went on strike in sympathy.

The great irony was that whilst the crisis was unfolding, a national settlement of the dispute was reached, brokered by Lloyd George at the Board of Trade. The strike was at an end.

The madness ended too and sense of shame descended on the town. The local Paper said '*Llanelli from now on will not be known as a peaceful town but as the abode of rioters, thieves and drunkards.*' So it did its best to try and wipe it away. Saturday 19 August 1911. A day to forget. The day that never happened.

As the years have gone on there has been greater willingness to engage with these shocking events. There is now a blue commemorative plaque at Union Bridge on Queen Victoria Road which marks the cutting where the train was stopped. The centenary was marked by rallies. There were speeches. And of course, there are the graves. They have been refurbished as part of a town's duty to its past. They can't be forgotten now. They are well-cared for. Often visited too – everyone knows how to find them. They are about 50 yards apart and the path between them is well worn. They will never slip into a comfortable obscurity.

Leonard's family could not afford a funeral, so the War Office kindly donated £4. Major Brownlow-Stuart was promoted and retired as a Brigadier-General in 1919. He died in 1952. The court returned verdicts of 'justifiable homicide.' Everything became ordered once more. But for a long time after these grim events, the Worcestershire cricket team was, by inevitable association, known locally as 'The Murderers'.

Llanidloes, Powys
The Onslow Brothers, 1921

In their death they were not divided

You will find their grave, perhaps a little neglected now, towards the back of the cemetery in Llanidloes. Leave the centre of the pretty market town and head north along the B4569. You will find the Dolhafren Cemetery on the right-hand side, after the hospital. Drive carefully through the arch in front of you and follow the main path down towards the bottom. There, on the left-hand side, you will find the low tomb of the Onslow Boys. A little battered and faded now, with their names on either side. They are remembered rarely and even when they are briefly considered today, it is not for what they did, but because of what happened to them, for this is a silent memorial to a notorious railway disaster.

The Onslow grave in Llanidloes

129

A little before midday on 26 January 1921 two trains were approaching Abermule from opposite directions and were due to pass each other there. There was a west bound stopping train from Whitchurch that had left at 10.05 am. And, heading east, there was the 10.25 am Aberystwyth express. The Onslow boys, Ralph Denzil, seventeen, and Guildford Dennis, sixteen, were on their way back to Harrow school from the family home near Llanidloes. Their brother was unwell with a bad dose of the 'flu but would join them later. They probably got on the Aberystwyth to Manchester express at Machynlleth to change at Shrewsbury for all stations south. Back to school to see their old friends. Back to the gossip. Back to the routine…They never made that connection. Instead their father, Richard Onslow, had to identify their bodies.

Because one mile south of Abermule the trains met each other. They became the twin halves of one awful event, brought together by an accumulation of mistakes and assumptions. This was the Abermule collision. Seventeen killed, thirty-six injured.

The papers described the scene in the midst of the quiet countryside as *'a gruesome silhouette of two trains inextricably mingled.'* It was an accident that should never have happened.

There is a very thorough report from the Public Safety and General Purposes Department at the Ministry of Transport which was written in April. Every aspect of the horrible collision is explored in detail. The condition of the trains examined forensically. *'The total overall length of the two trains was about 252 yards. After the collision the space occupied, including wrecked stock, was 180 yards.'* Seventy yards of machinery had just disappeared into a tangled mass. It had to be cut up before it could be taken away. Nine of the coaches were lit by gas and it was a matter of some relief that there was no explosion. At least the water from the engines had put out the boiler fires. The last coaches of each train were largely undamaged. It was the front parts that had disappeared. *'Smashed carriages, broken glass, upholstery with sinister stains lay about.'*

Tyers No. 6 Electric Train Tablet System, designed to maintain safety on a single line of track, was efficient and effective. *'If the instruments are used fairly, and in accordance with instructions, the possibility of accident has been considered so remote as to be negligible.'*

Absolutely right. It didn't fail. It was the people who failed. Railway employees displayed what the report called *'Indiscipline and slipshod methods.'*

The tablet system was a simple but ingenious concept. Two linked machines stood at the opposite ends of a section of single track. A driver would be given a tablet from the machine which gave him the authorisation to proceed. Until he had deposited it at the other end, no one else could use that length of track. Not a problem. Except that in Abermule station, things had been a bit lax of late. Only the stationmaster was supposed to deal with the procedure. But over time, procedures had slipped. It had become a job for anyone who happened to be around.

Of course they blamed the staffing levels. Things haven't changed that much.

'The recent reduction in railwaymen's hours of working, the necessity for avoiding overtime, and for economy in working have…caused alterations both in the number of personnel employed on traffic duties and in the arrangement of those duties.'

The report however contradicts this. It indicated that there had been an increase in staff since the end of the war. The amount of traffic (twenty-two trains per day) was not *'of such frequency as to prevent the regulations in connection with the custody and transference of tablets from being given full effect to by the stationmaster.'* It wasn't anything to do with staffing. They just got it horribly wrong.

As it was, an unauthorised person, a porter called Ernest Percy Rogers, *'a lad of 17'*, took a tablet from the machine and gave it to the wrong person. He never stopped to examine what he was doing. Why should he? He knew what to do, even if this wasn't

131

technically part of his job. He had picked up procedures from watching others. No one checked. Human error. Meant that the wrong tablet was given to a person who never checked it.

So the tablet was passed from hand to hand but never checked or treated properly. No one took responsibility to check anything because they assumed that someone else had. If they had bothered to check it would have shown them that the express was on its way and had right of way.

Driver Jones was oiling his engine when the tablet was handed to Fireman Evans. Driver Jones never checked that he had been given the correct tablet. Why should he? Fireman Evans had received it from the staff at Abermule. They knew what they were doing. It had never been a problem before.

However, procedures had been followed correctly at Newtown. The express train built up speed as it headed towards Abermule. They had authorisation. No one had told them that the stopping train was on its way.

So, whereas the trains were due to pass each other safely at 12.05 pm, with the stopping train waiting on a loop of line for the express to pass at 50 mph, at 12.06 pm they found themselves on the same line heading towards each other.

Driver Jones and Fireman Evans of the stopping train were travelling along confidently, though much more slowly, at about 20 mph. They also believed that the track was theirs.

It does not appear as if they were ever aware of what was going on. They certainly didn't apply their brakes at all. They probably didn't even see the express that was hurtling towards them. As they say, they didn't know what hit them.

They were both killed.

'The engine of the express mounted the engine of the local train and crashed on the roof of the first coach and remained suspended.'

The driver and fireman of the express, John Pritchard Jones and John Owen, had sounded their whistle and applied the brakes as soon as they saw the other train. They managed to reduce their speed from 50 mph to 30 mph. But there was no way of avoiding the collision. They jumped from their engine just before impact. In the first carriage, in the vicious telescoping metal, the Onslow Boys were killed. Lord Herbert Vane-Tempest, a director of the Cambrian Railways, died in hospital later. He was *'dragged from the very bottom of the debris'* along with his valet.

The majority of the fatalities were local people, united in death with a travelling salesman from Manchester and a lady from Birmingham. It was an awful scene, and it is interesting to note that the witnesses and the reporters use military imagery to try and describe what they saw. All they could draw upon were their experiences of war in the trenches. The two trains for example, *'looked as if they had been shelled by heavy guns.'* To another, the scene was worse than anything he had seen on medical duty in France. *'The shrieks and cries of the dying and injured were heartrending.'*

The first thing that Owen did was to crawl over to Jones to check whether they had the right of way. After all, the regulations stated clearly that it was the engine driver's responsibility to *'assure himself of the correctness of the token.'* But they had not done anything wrong. Pritchard Jones was a meticulous man. He had worked for the company for twenty-nine years and as a driver for fourteen. This was his life.

'I have never known in my experience that a driver has failed to recognise the responsibility laid upon him for examining the tablet himself.'

Jones always needed to check the token himself. Others were clearly much more casual.

Owen later recovered the tablet from underneath the wreckage to comfort his distressed colleague. Jones needed to know that he hadn't made a mistake. Of course, it was the right tablet. There was never a problem with procedures in Newtown or on Jones' footplate. It was in Abermule where *'practice was slipshod.'*

Without *'absolute obedience'* to procedures, then the system would always remain vulnerable. It was not the machine that changed procedures. A machine is designed to repeat a process regularly and without variation; it is people who get it wrong.

And no matter how thorough an enquiry, no matter how many statements were taken, no matter how many recommendations would be made, a mother had to bury two sons.

'Their father and mother heard of the disaster and motored to Newtown, where they learned that one of the boys had been killed. Half an hour afterwards the second son's body was recovered. The grief of the parents was pathetic.'

She arrived at the committal in the quiet stillness of Llanidloes in her yellow Rolls Royce, in the bright clothes that her sons always admired. The final gesture of a devoted mother.

Around the base of the grave there is the lament of David over the death of Saul and his son Jonathan, in the Second Book of Samuel.

They were lovely and pleasant in their lives

and in their death, they were not divided.

The language of the official report into the institutional carelessness that led to the collision, distances the reader from the genuine human tragedy of what happened. Two young boys on their way back to school were part of the casualty list. Lives snuffed out in an instant. It did not matter how well connected the boys were, whether or not their mother turned up at the cemetery in a posh car. They may have come from an influential family, with their wealth based upon lead mining. They may have lived on a country estate at Mount Severn.

None of that matters. Everything they represented ended at that moment.

Meidrim, Carmarthenshire
Ira Jones, 1960

Pease Let Me Do This Forever

Drive along the A40 out of Carmarthen towards St. Clears and then take the turning to Meidrim. And there, where the B4298 meets it, you will find Ira Jones, finally resting in a small graveyard at the junction. It is in the top corner, up against the wall. This is where the fighter ace finally came to ground.

In proud and loving memory of
Wing Commander
James Ira Thomas Jones
1896 – 1960
Gay and Gallant, he fought for Christian Principles.

Of course, given the way he lived his life, it is hard to know where to find the 'Christian Principles' with which he fought, but perhaps these are merely words from another time. For Ira Jones, there was always the sense of freedom in the sky, above the cloying mud of the battlefield, unconfined by the boundaries of those below. For a while he was a national hero, defending the country, not as a member of an army, but alone, pitting his wits against a merciless enemy in single combat. To kill or be killed.

To abandon such limitless possibilities and return to earth at the end of the war was always going to be difficult. And it is clear that Ira never found anything that could ever replace the raw excitement and terror of those days when he fought and killed in the skies.

I looked up into the limitless blue kingdom of the sky, and I prayed, 'Oh God, please let me do this forever.'

There is also a fine memorial to him in the centre of St. Clears, by the side of the river, erected in 1964 by public subscription. It reads, *In proud memory of Group Captain James Ira T. Jones.*

Oh yes, Ira was a hero. A hero from a different time.

Ira Jones was born in April 1896 in Llanddowror, just outside St. Clears, where his mother later ran the sweet shop. He was illegitimate and this, along with his short stature and his stammer, made life difficult for him at school.

He went to Glasfryn Council school and then to the Queen Elizabeth Grammar School in Carmarthen, where he spent all his time fighting and playing rugby. Prompted, he said, by the news of the sinking of the *Titanic*, he announced he was going to be a radio operator. His mother was less convinced by such uncertain career opportunities and got him a job in the land valuation office. But he continued to study wireless and cable telegraphy. A career in the Civil Service seemed far too safe.

He joined the Territorial Army in 1913, since the regular army wouldn't have him, and then volunteered for the Royal Flying Corps, becoming firstly an air mechanic, then an observer and then, finally, in May 1917 he did his pilot training. He was assigned to 74 Squadron and sent out to fly above the Western Front along the French and Belgian border. He was just another young man, sent out to fly a plane. Whatever talent he had was less important than willingness, for pilots were not expected to survive for long. The life expectancy of a pilot on the Western Front was about six weeks.

But Ira Jones had three invaluable qualities. He possessed real ability as a pilot, he was courageous and, most importantly, he was lucky.

136

Ira had the unfortunate habit of crashing his planes on landing, but never suffered any serious injury. He survived 28 crashes, The ground they landed on was merely poorly prepared pasture, more suited to cows than machines, but his shape was perhaps the most important detail. He had short legs which he could tuck up underneath him and, in this way, escape serious injury in a collapsing cockpit. Many others were less fortunate.

Injury, death and heroism were part of his daily experience, and Ira was always brave and he was also an excellent pilot.

When they made him Flight Commander, he never lost a man on any patrol that he led. It was important to him. He had suddenly found the thing that he could do and he did it very well.

His whole life soon became defined by an explosive burst of glory in 1918 when, for a brief period, he was a national hero. He scored thirty-seven victories in just three months. It was an intense, adrenaline - fuelled period when, every day, Ira himself could have been killed. The longer he went unscathed, the greater the statistical prospect of his own destruction became.

There are many myths about the pilots, about their code of chivalry and their honour. But the reality of killing in the sky had no such dignity. Success, and thus self-preservation, involved attacking your opponent without warning from above. The great British fighter ace and Ira's great friend, Mick Mannock, was deeply afraid of being shot down in flames - becoming a "Flamer" – so he carried a loaded pistol out on patrol to use on himself if his aircraft started to burn. He was, of course, quite happy to consign a German to this awful fate. He wrote, 'Sizzle sizzle. I sent one of the bastards to hell in flames today.' Mannock died when he circled in triumph above the burning wreck of a German plane and was shot down by machine gun fire from the ground. The pilot Ira admired most of all, killed by earth-bound soldiers.

Ira had a naïve, unquestioning patriotism. His contempt for the enemy was boundless, and he was quite happy to write about how

137

he shot and killed German pilots parachuting to safety. In these circumstances, life was for the lucky and, beyond anything else, Ira was lucky. The longer he survived, the more medals he was awarded and the more his celebrity grew.

But however personal duels in the air might be presented as the expression of an ancient code of chivalry, it was a vicious business. Pilots were taught never to attack a plane from behind. All they would ever achieve was to fill the body of the observer in the rear seat with bullets and his body would then protect that of the pilot in front. Fly too close and your windscreen will be obscured by his blood.

It was in such an environment that Ira fought and survived.

On 3 August 1918 he was cited for the DFC – for attacking and destroying six enemy aircraft and displaying *great courage, skill and initiative.'* In September he was cited for the MC – for *'gallantry and devotion to duty.'* And then he was awarded the bar to his DFC for being a *'gallant officer.'* The DSO? He got that for *'skilful tactics and marksmanship, with high courage.'*

Perhaps his greatest achievement was that he endured. But the greatest period of his life lasted for only four months, and then it was over. The rest of his life happened in the shadow of those days.

Ira went on to fight in Russia in the British intervention in the civil war but it was not a happy experience. Poorly equipped, he improvised by dropping empty beer bottles on the opposition. But Ira was no longer a hero and, more importantly, he was no longer sure what he was fighting for. He was a forgotten man, flying aimlessly above the endless forests of Northern Russia for which he received Russian Order of St. George.

He then served in Iraq, dropping bombs on tribesmen, but soon returned to a life in the Civil Service, this time working for the Ministry of Pensions. How could this ever compete with the life he had once had? In his spare time, he leant against numerous bars.

He was recalled as an instructor in 1939 and appointed as a Wing Commander. But instructing was always going to be too tame. Once he flew after a German bomber from his base in Swansea, armed only with a pistol. Bravado? To those around him, he was yesterday's man and his heavy drinking led to his demobilisation. From hero to embarrassment.

He wrote about his career in *'An Air Fighter's Scrapbook'* and in *'Tiger Squadron,'* books which are remarkable for their insight and candour. They give a genuine picture of what it was like to wake up, believing that today you would burn to death in a fragile aircraft, tumbling to the ground.

Ira was, for a time, rugby correspondent for the *'Sunday Dispatch.'* Any player, no matter how average, could get a mention in the report, just as long as they bought him enough whisky. He once stole a steam train from Cardiff station and set off down the line. But these were small thrills.

Eventually, he became involved in one of Dylan Thomas' notorious drinking escapades, at the Pentre Arms in Llangrannog. Together, they decided to help themselves to drink from behind the bar and the landlord, Tom Jones, physically removed them both from the pub.

Do you know who we are? shouted Ira.

Such a silly question, for you are never likely to appreciate the answer. And so it proved.

I don't care, said Jones, as he banned them.

The currency of his past was no longer relevant; his time had been and gone. Old glories and triumphs no longer mattered.

Ira Jones, the fighter ace, lost the liberty of the blues skies that had defined him and he died, prosaically, when he tripped over a step in August 1960.

Today we can find him confined within a newly restored grave, inside that red brick boundary. A man of his time. No longer free.

Ira Jones, down to earth

Newport
John Byrne VC, 1879

A fighter, not a soldier

In war, it often comes down to survival of the fittest, especially when the fighting becomes personal, when you stare into the eyes of your enemy and you try to kill each other. The fittest is often the brutal killer, the one without compassion or understanding.

This one was a brute, he was a killer and he was very good at it, so they gave him a VC. Say a big hello then, to John Byrne.

Remembered as a hero. Forgotten as a man

There are obvious similarities between John Byrne and Charles Lumley, one of the other Crimea veterans buried here in Wales and who features in this book in the entry for Brecon.

141

They may have come from entirely different ends of the social spectrum, but both were awarded the Victoria Cross for their bravery in the Crimea. And they both eventually shot themselves in the head. But they arrived at their unfortunate and sad deaths by entirely different routes.

John Byrne was an ill-disciplined brawler. He was a fighter, not a soldier. But it was this that won him his Victoria Cross and his DCM.

He was born in 1832 and was an uneducated boy from Kilkenny in Ireland. Like so many others, he came to England to escape poverty and famine at home. He had no job and no skills. What could he do? So he enlisted in the 68th Regiment of Foot in 1850 in Coventry. He did not find military life easy. In 1853 he was sent to a military prison for the first time, sentenced to six months. He was released in May 1854 and by July was back inside again. We can only speculate about what he did, but his subsequent record would suggest that there was probably fighting involved somewhere, along with the drinking of extreme amounts of alcohol.

John Byrne was released from prison in August but only because his regiment was off to the Crimea. This was probably his salvation. This opportunity to kill others was what put his military career on track.

If he was in the army, at least he was out of the pubs and off the streets. But John Byrne's saving grace was his highly developed sense of loyalty to his comrades, which was perfectly illustrated at the Battle of Inkerman in November 1854. The initial attack by the Russians threatened to overrun the British divisions, and soldiers were sent almost at random into the line to halt the assault. The terrain was rough and a fog had settled over the battlefield. The British were fighting in small groups against unknown numbers of the enemy who they couldn't see. It was unstructured hand-to-hand fighting, not the neat formations of the parade ground; it was a pub fight, but without the rules; it was the perfect situation for someone like Byrne.

As the British began to abandon their wounded and were driven backwards, he saw Private Anthony Harman lying on the ground. Byrne rushed straight into the Russian fire to rescue him. He picked him up and carried him back. This was probably the first time in his life he had done something that didn't get him into trouble. It was an instinctive act of heroism that was noted.

The winter was appalling and the troops lived without proper shelter or equipment, but they did manage to push their network of trenches closer to the defences of their main objective, Sebastopol. Such advances unsettled the defenders and on 11 May 1855 a large force of Russians left the city and attacked the British trenches in fierce driving rain. Once again, it was brutal, hand-to-hand fighting. At one point Byrne became involved with a Russian on the trench parapet and stabbed him with his bayonet and seized his musket. The struggle was witnessed by many and felt to have inspired the British troops, who drove the Russians back into the city.

Once again, Byrne had succeeded in a situation that called upon his own instincts, rather than his training. This action, together with the incident at Inkerman, led to the award of the Victoria Cross and eventually his promotion to Corporal. He was unable to receive the award from the Queen herself in London, instead it was presented to him in Corfu where the regiment was stationed.

In late 1863 they were posted to New Zealand to deal with land disputes between the European settlers and the Maoris that had escalated into open warfare. Here Byrne was involved in the Battle of Te Ranga, near Tauranga, in June 1864.

The Regiment attacked an unfinished defensive structure called a "pah", or fort, and again, vicious hand-to-hand fighting ensued. Byrne was the first man of his company to jump into the enemy rifle pits, where he immediately impaled a Maori soldier with his bayonet. But he didn't fall down, and this left Byrne with something of a problem.

The Maori grabbed Byrne's rifle with one hand and started to thrash away with his war axe with the other. The only thing that could keep his enemy at a distance was the rifle and Byrne could not let go. If he stayed as he was, then he had no means of finishing the fight or protecting himself from the thrashing axe. A dance of death, Maori and Irishman, together in an infernal and deathly union.

He was rescued by Sergeant John Murray, another Crimea veteran. He had been fighting his way through the Maoris in the fire pit. He himself had already killed or wounded twelve defenders with his bayonet and he quickly dealt with Byrne's opponent.

Murray thus won a VC for his actions, including rescuing a VC. Byrne was awarded the Distinguished Conduct Medal for leading the charge.

The rest of John Byrne's life was, sadly, far less distinguished. When the regiment returned to England in 1866, he was promoted to Sergeant. He stayed with them until 1872, when he took his discharge after twenty-one years of service. He never married; he had no children. The 68th Regiment had been his life. Without the structure it provided however, his life became shapeless.

He joined the Durham Militia as a Colour Sergeant but was discharged within a few months for *'insubordination and highly improper conduct.'* It is easy to speculate that his temper and his drinking were to blame.

The next reference to him is in 1878 when he was working as a labourer for Ordnance Survey in Bristol. He told his landlady there, that he had lost all his possessions, including his medals, in a house fire in Cork. Later in the year, he was moved by the Survey to Newport, where he lodged at 7 Crown Street, Maindee.

On 10 July 1879, he got into an argument with a colleague

called John Watts, who was only 19. Byrne accused him of insulting the Victoria Cross, though I think we can imagine that the young man might have been rather dismissive of someone who claimed to have won the very highest award, and yet couldn't show it. This boastful older man, a bit of a drunk, working as a labourer, a hero? Don't make me laugh.

The next day Byrne turned up at work with a gun. As they assembled, he shot Watts once in the shoulder and ran away. It was a slight wound, but a wound nonetheless. Watts was lucky he didn't bring a bayonet.

Later that day a policeman called at Byrne's lodging to question him. Byrne drew his gun once more but instead of shooting the officer, he put it in his own mouth and pulled the trigger.

He died instantly. He was 46 years old.

Who can say what was going on inside his head? A sense of futility? A sense that he was forever condemned to work with irritating little boys who would never be able to spear a fish, let alone spear a man? That all his achievements and purpose had ended when he stepped out of that rifle pit in New Zealand? All we can say is that the anger and the lack of control that won him his medals, just as certainly brought him to his death.

There are no photographs of John Byrne, the hero who was buried in an unmarked pauper's grave in St Woolo's Cemetery in Newport on 12 July 1879. Outside of limited military circles, he soon became a forgotten man. He left nothing and no one after him, other than his medal citations. He sank out of sight.

But at least some redress has been made. A headstone for him was eventually dedicated in November 1985, when a wreath was laid by Major-General de la Billiere. It is this stone that you can now see on the lawn cemetery there.

John Byrne's life was defined by fighting and conflict. When that wasn't needed anymore what was left? Perhaps there is indeed nobility and self-sacrifice in war. But perhaps these qualities are nowhere near as important as brutality and viciousness. And when John Byrne had a bayonet on the end of his rifle, he had plenty.

Newtown, Powys
Robert Owen 1858

---

*A grave is too cold and damp, for a soul so warm
and true.*

---

*The stone over his grave in the old churchyard was a very plain structure and
the spot presented a very desolate and deserted appearance. Now all is changed,
and henceforth Wales will have something worthy of the man to remind her of
one of its noblest sons.*

Thankfully we can still see the benefits of this work today. On
Saturday 12 July 1902 *'co-operators from all parts of the country'* met in
St Mary's churchyard in Newtown, to honour the memory of
Robert Owen and the restoration of his tomb. A job well done.
Railings. Inscription. Image. Frieze. All for Robert Owen. All
deserved.

The Owen family tomb

Does this grave contain the body of the greatest Welshman of them all? That is what some people believe. Without doubt, he was one of the most significant figures of the nineteenth century. Socialist, philanthropist, visionary, co-operator – he was all of these – and more. Owen was born in Newtown, he was buried in Newtown and his alternative social vision has reached out across the world, touching the lives of millions. There are those who know of him, who know nothing of Wales.

He was born in 1771 and was the sixth of seven children. Like so many people, his intellectual liberation came through reading and the emancipation that education and reading could bring was an idea which never left him.

At the age of ten he left home with his eldest brother William and found a job as an apprentice in a drapery business in Stamford. This simple step formed the whole direction of his life. He took up a similar post in London and then, when he was sixteen, he moved to Manchester.

He found himself, quite by chance, in a hub of the industrial revolution, at a key moment in its development. He was quick to seize an opportunity and, with money borrowed from William, he established a business manufacturing machine tools – making the machines that made the cotton – and then he put the knowledge he had acquired to practical use, by setting up as a cotton spinner, soon winning a reputation amongst his peers for producing fine yarns.

He eventually became a partner in the Chorlton Twist Company, which purchased mills in New Lanark near Glasgow from David Dale. These mills employed over 1500 people, including 500 children, and by 1800 it was the largest cotton-spinning development in the country. David Dale was regarded as a progressive employer, concerned to protecting the well-being of children and he had been keen to sell the mills to someone who shared the same commitment. Children were frequently killed or seriously injured in industrial accidents, and there was increasing unease at their exploitation. Dale found that person in Robert Owen, who went on to marry his daughter, Caroline.

The emphasis at New Lanark on the well-being of workers established Owen's reputation as a philanthropist. He was responsible for introducing increased hygiene standards and for the development of an infant school and a store. He won the trust of his workers by continuing to pay them for 4 months when cotton production stopped in most mills, during the 1806 American embargo on exports. Owen didn't just talk about his ideals. He did practical things to make things better for others.

I arranged superior stores and shops, from which to supply every article of food, clothing etc. which they required. I bought everything in the first markets on a large scale and had articles of the best quality supplied to the people at cost price. This saved them full twenty-five per cent. The effects soon became visible in their improved health and superior dress, and in the general comfort of their houses.

This was an alternative to the 'truck system.' Some employers paid their workers, not with currency but with tokens, a system endemic in the ironworks in Wales. These tokens had no value at all, except in the owner's 'truck shop'. Consequently, they could sell second-rate produce and charge high prices to workers who had little or no choice about where they could shop. This was a notorious abuse which was eventually banned by Parliament. It was Robert Owen who showed them the way. In his stores workers had access to good quality goods at wholesale cost. These principles underpinned the subsequent growth of the co-operative movement and it is one of the reasons why Owen has been so highly regarded.

He promoted the idea of the eight-hour day, with the slogan: *'Eight hours labour, Eight hours recreation, Eight hours rest,'* which seems a reasonable way of organising your time.

He also developed a self-monitored system to measure workers performance, called the *'silent monitor,'* which was a concept a long way ahead of its time. He removed threats and intimidation as a means of improving performance, replacing it with a sense of pride in a job done properly. The *'silent monitor'* was a four-sided piece of wood which hung prominently at a work-station, each side a different colour. The side displayed the colour which corresponded to the workers performance the previous day. Black signified bad, blue meant indifferent, yellow represented good and white excellent. The colour displayed effectively projected your performance and your self-worth to the world. Owen observed that, *'It was gratifying to observe the new spirit created by these silent monitors. At the commencement, the great majority were black; they were gradually succeeded by blue, and then by yellow, and some white.'* Truly a triumph of management.

New Lanark attracted much attention with a stream of prominent visitors, and Owen continued to develop his belief in *'villages of co-operation'* when he bought New Harmony in Indiana in America, where he hoped the workers would eventually become a self-governing community. It was an alternative image of social development. There was agriculture, small industries and community buildings and, for a while, Owen travelled between the two communities in America and Scotland. However, whilst many went there, not all the new residents of New Harmony had the skills required to generate an income. Sadly the project ultimately failed.

Back in Scotland, despite the fact that business prospered, he faced constant opposition from his partners. Eventually Owen ended his connection with New Lanark in 1828. His said to a partner, William Allen, *'All the world is queer save thee and me, and even thou art a little queer.'* a point of view with which I have always had some sympathy.

Owen remained convinced that an individual's character was formed entirely by the effects of their environment. Education would create rational and humane individuals and thus establish an environment in which a child could develop under what he regarded as proper influences. Education was always at the heart of all his beliefs.

He opened the National Equitable Labour Exchange where 'labour notes' valued in hours could be exchanged for merchandise and he became involved in the developing trade union movement. His commitment to radical socialist ideals remained constant right up to his death.

Returning to Newtown from a meeting in Liverpool, he fell ill whilst staying at the Bear Hotel. In the evening he asked the Rector to convene a meeting at which he would speak on the necessary reform of education but died the next morning, 17 November 1858. Despite the protests of supporters, he was given a Christian burial.

On the ground floor of the Council Offices in Newtown there is the fine Robert Owen Museum which is essential for all visitors to Newtown. It gives a fascinating picture of a committed and influential man. The plaster cast of the 'life mask' they have there, made when Owen was fifty, brings you closer to the reality the man behind the vision.

His grave which he shares with his parents, Anne and Robert, has been twice restored. It was surrounded by fine ornate railings erected by the Co-operative Movement in 1902, which give it the prominence the grave deserves and it was all spruced up again in 1993. You can find the tomb in the churchyard of St Mary's in the middle of Newtown and there is a fine statue too, erected in 1956 in a garden on Shortbridge Street. There is also a copy of this statue outside the Co-operative Bank headquarters on Balloon Street in Manchester.

Robert Owen had a paternalistic desire to influence and improve the lives of others by promoting combination of co-operation and self-help. In some ways he remained a paradox - he was a successful capitalist who believed in worker control – but he never lost his belief in the essential goodness of humanity. As it says on his tomb, *It is the one great universal interest of the human race to be cordially united and to aid each other to the full extent of their capacities.'*

On Shortbridge Street in Newtown and Balloon Street in Manchester

But it seems to me that the most touching words of all were those of his friends, who said on his death, *a grave is too cold and damp for a soul so warm and true.*

St Clears, Carmarthenshire

Frederick Higginson 2003

Saved by Chocolate

St Clears is a lovely place, certainly on a sunny day. So go there. Head towards Laugharne and on the left-hand side you will find your destination, the Church of Mary Magdalene. It is opposite the historic Town Hall and you will pass through a beautiful lych gate into a tranquil timeless world. The church has a long history. It was founded in 1100 as a priory and apparently contains the best Norman stone carving in Carmarthenshire. And yet in all that time there can have been no one buried there who has had such a dramatic life as the man whose grave you have come to see.

An expression of the undying love they shared, in Welsh

153

It isn't difficult to find. It is a modern headstone erected in 2003 and it shines brightly on the left-hand side as you walk down the path towards the church. It is a stone which summarises a life but which is unable to give you a full picture of the quite remarkable career of Wing Commander Frederick Higginson OBE DFC DFM (1913-2003), fighter ace. As you will see, if anyone lived a life which might have been scripted for them in Hollywood, then it was 'Taffy' Higginson.

He was born in Gorseinon near Swansea in 1913, joined the RAF as an apprentice in 1929 and was accepted for pilot training in 1935. He was a young man living a dream but all too soon he was experiencing a nightmare. By 1940 he had been promoted to Flight Sergeant and was fighting over Dunkirk before moving on to the Battle of Britain over the green fields of Kent. He was awarded the DFM and became one of only thirty-six British fighter pilots during the whole of World War II to shoot down more than twelve enemy aircraft - and this at a time when government planners estimated the average life expectancy of a fighter pilot at only three weeks.

However, Higginson ran out of luck whilst escorting a formation of Blenheim bombers raiding Lille in June 1941. His Hurricane was hit by a cannon shell and spiralled out of control near St Omer. He parachuted out and the adventure began.

'I pulled the rip-cord, the parachute opened, and after the tremendous noise all was peace and quiet. The countryside below looked delightful in the summer sunshine.'

He floated gently into a wood northwest of Fauquembergues, where he was detained by a German officer and sergeant who had watched his peaceful descent from their motorbike and sidecar. With considerable professional pride they stuffed their prize capture into the sidecar. But they couldn't pull their eyes away from the drama of the skies above them and so, when they were distracted by a low-flying German fighter, Higginson grabbed hold of the handlebars, over-turned the vehicle into a ditch and disappeared into the woods. Suddenly he was on the run.

Higginson was picked up by the French Resistance and taken to Captain Harold 'Paul' Cole, apparently a survivor of Dunkirk and local co-ordinator of the underground escape route. Cole took him to a priest, Abbé Carpentier in Abbeville, where he was provided with false identity papers. Higginson then travelled to Paris where he lodged in a brothel for a month waiting for escape procedures to be finalised. The established escape route was into Vichy France and then over the Pyrenees into Spain and so Cole escorted Higginson to the south. Everything went to plan until they were questioned by a pair of German soldiers at the station in St Martin le Beau.

Despite his best efforts, the soldiers were strangely unimpressed by Cole's explanation that Higginson was a mentally-impaired relative looking for work, a deception designed to hide his limited language skills. But when the soldiers searched his suitcase, their examination was little more than cursory. They were reluctant to explore its contents, which were covered in chocolate that had melted in the summer heat. When Cole opened his own bag, they failed to discover a pistol and incriminating documents which had been hidden in tangles of dirty laundry, and so they were sent on their way.

Once they entered Vichy France, Higginson made his way to Marseilles, where he was accommodated in a safe house for a while. However he was impatient to get home and so caught a train to Perpignan where, with a disguised Australian Army corporal, he hired a local Catalan guide to take them across the border to Spain. It was not a success. When they were stopped by gendarmes, Higginson, in his frustration, hit one of them. This was not wise. He was imprisoned for six months for having false papers.

In March 1942 he was about to be released, when he was further detained in reprisal for an air raid on the Renault factory at

Billancourt. He was then imprisoned in Fort de la Revere above Monte Carlo. Conditions were dreadful and his weight fell from eleven stones to seven.

Back in London the authorities were very keen to be reunited with a valuable resource. A pilot with his exceptional record was an asset they needed desperately. Consequently, he became part of the Special Operations Executive plan '*Titania,*' designed to recover allied airmen. Father Myrda, a Polish priest, smuggled a hacksaw blade into the prison and on 6 August 1942 Higginson and four others - under the cover of a diversionary and noisy prison concert - dropped through a coal chute, down into a moat and out through a sewage pipe to a safe house. Perhaps the weight loss was useful, after all.

Then, disguised as priests, Father Myrda took the group to Marseilles and handed them over to the French resistance who took them to Canet Plage, near Perpignan. In September the group were picked up from the beach by a dingy, taken out to a Polish fishing trawler and then transferred to a SOE fast patrol boat, *HMS Minna*. This took them to Gibraltar, from where Higginson was flown home to RAF Greenock on 5 October 1942 to join a Typhoon squadron. Soon he was fighting in the skies once more, his skills undiminished. A year later in 1943 he awarded Distinguished Flying Cross.

What an adventure. Sadly, Paul Cole who had escorted him into Vichy France and to whom he owed so much, was not what he seemed. He was not a stranded Army captain at all but a sergeant who had deserted during the retreat to Dunkirk, together with mess funds and had gone into hiding. Furthermore, under interrogation by the Germans, Cole had betrayed members of the escape organisation, including Abbe Carpentier who was then executed.

After the war Higginson was promoted to Wing commander and was involved in staff training until he retired from the RAF in

1956. He worked at Bristol Aircraft Company as its military liaison officer and then as sales and service director of the Guided Missiles Division. His work in developing overseas markets for guided weapons systems like the Bloodhound ground-to-air missile was recognised with an OBE. Frederick Higginson never lost contact with his past and always retained a respect for the German pilots who had once tried to shoot him down, fighting for their country just as he had fought for his.

When he retired, he learned about farming with the same enthusiasm that he learned to fly and moved to a large estate at Penycoed in Carmarthenshire. He lived there with his wife Jenny "Shan" Jenkins, whom he had married in 1937, and their four sons. He died aged 89 in February 2003, a few months after Shan, following a mercifully quick decline. And when he was buried in St Mary Parish Church in St Clears, his achievements were recognised by an RAF fly-past, honouring the remarkable story of a man who was truly one of their own.

Swansea, Mynyddbach

Daniel James, 1920

Calon Lân

The grave of Daniel James

Mynyddbach Chapel is lovely. It is a small comfortable place, an archetypal Welsh Chapel, the oldest Independent chapel in Swansea. and you can find it set back from Llangyfelach Road in Treboeth. It was built in 1867, renovated in the middle of the twentieth century and threatened with demolition in the twenty first. It was saved by a group of local activists and we owe them a debt of gratitude, not only for the preservation of a lovely chapel, but also for saving one of Swansea's most important graves, which resides in its cemetery, one which has such significance across the country. Within it rests the poet Daniel James, who wrote the words of the hymn, Calon Lân, regarded as the second National Anthem of Wales. His story is a fascinating one, one of unexpected contrasts, of achievement and tragedy, and one which provides an unexpected insight into the lives and tribulations of ordinary people in industrial South Wales during the latter part of the nineteenth century.

Daniel James was born in 1848 in Treboeth in Swansea, where the family were members of Mynyddbach Chapel. They were a large family living in a small cottage, like so many others, and their expectations of what life might offer them. probably did not extend beyond the one lived by their parents. Daniel's formal education was inevitably minimal, although it is believed that he briefly attended a local drama school. Sadly his education – and his childhood - were terminated when his father died unexpectedly and, in 1861, at the age of 13, Daniel began work as a labourer in the Landore Tinplate Works, eventually attaining skilled positions like that of puddler and traffic manager. He was employed there for thirty-three years until it closed in 1894.

Away from work he mastered the intricate formalities of Welsh poetry. He was taught by D.W. Thomas, an elder at Mynyddbach Chapel, and began to write verse initially as '*Dafydd Mynyddbach*', and then later he assumed the Bardic name '*Gwyrosydd*'.

In 1871, at the age of 23 Daniel married Ann Hopkin and they lived in Treboeth, having five children. In the locality he developed a reputation as an enthusiastic drinker. Neighbours, struggling perhaps to reconcile his attendance in chapel with his attendance in public houses, said of him that he would have '*sold his soul for a pint of beer.*' He was particularly fond of the King's Head. where he would sit at the bar on an unusually high chair, now on proud display in the chapel, composing poems and rhymes in exchange for drinks. He would also turn up at weddings and compose a poem in honour of the happy couple, managing his thirst in return for carefully chosen words.

Poems came to order from The Big Chair

For many working-class families, living precarious lives on the very edge of poverty and ruin, tragedy was a constant companion. You can see this very clearly in Daniel James' life. His wife Ann, the woman who would sometimes not let Daniel back into the house after his drinking sessions, thus forcing him to sleep in the pigsty, sadly died on Christmas Eve, 1887. He was suddenly a 40-year-old widower with five young children. For our ancestors there was little time for sentimentality. If he found no one to look after the children, then he couldn't go to work - and so how would they live?

In October 1888 he married Gwenllian Parry, herself a widow with five children of her own. She had returned from Russia where her husband had died, possibly working at Yuzovka, an industrial centre established by Welshman John Hughes in what is today Donetsk. The marriage was a mutually supportive contract which suited them both as single parents and they went on to have three more children together. It was a large family to support and when, in 1894 the Landore works closed down, the new James family had no alternative but to move around in search of work. They went to the Cynon valley, then to Tredegar and on to Dowlais. Daniel James spent some time working as a miner at Mountain Ash, until moving once more, this time to Blaengarw. This was, of course, in no way unusual and neither was the pressing need to get your children out to work as soon as possible, in order to boost the family income. It is what happened to him, but of course it came with its own dangers and had its own impact upon future opportunities.

They lived at No 8 Herbert St, Blaengarw, where Gwenllian gave birth to their last child, a son called Tawe James in 1895, but she died shortly afterward. The baby was sent away to live with Daniel's sister, Marged, in Llangyfelach. How else was the child to be cared for?

Amongst the tragedy, his second marriage had been a productive time for his poetry. Two collections were published, *'Caniadau Gwyrosydd'*, 1892 (which included Calon Lân) and *'Caneuon Cymru'* in 1895. The third collection *'Aeron Awen Gwyrosydd,'* appeared in 1898.

Tragedy though, would not leave Daniel James alone. His son, William, a miner, died after an incident in the pit. He developed tetanus following a minor foot injury which had become infected with horse manure that was stuck to a rope and he died a few days later. His body was returned to Mynyddbach, where it was interred alongside that of his mother.

Throughout his life, Daniel James had no alternative but to support his large family by working in difficult and often dangerous jobs. But he paid a heavy price for this and his health, like that of so many others, suffered considerably. It was not until 1916 that, aged 68, he finally retired from mining. Even then he took another the job, this time as cemetery caretaker and gravedigger at Mountain Ash.

He did eventually return to Swansea when he could no longer work. He ended his days in Swansea and died on 11 March 1920. He is buried at Mynyddbach along with his first wife Ann and his son William. They were later joined by his daughter Mary. As you approach the chapel you will see the extensive cemetery on the left and there are small wooden indicators which will direct you to his grave.

But what about his most famous work, Calon Lân? It is a poem which became a hymn and has generated so many myths. In the first place, no one can be sure where it was written. There are many who believe – or at least would like to believe – that Daniel James wrote the words on the back of a cigarette packet in Blaengarw. Neither is it clear where and when he met John Hughes, the man who gave Calon Lân its beautiful and simple melody, so easily sung, who is probably the one most responsible for its enduring success. There is a story of James thrusting the poem at Hughes as he walked home briskly from chapel one afternoon. He was unimpressed, more excited by the prospect of his tea than by unsolicited literary achievement. But there was something about the words which spoke to him, because at evening service he gave Daniel James the finished hymn.

Calon Lân has been sung to at least four different tunes and indeed can be adjusted to fit in with many others, but it is the power of the music composed by John Hughes which reaches out to people. No English Language version of the hymn is sung with any regularity, although there is, I am told, a Spanish version which, not surprisingly, is popular in Patagonia.

Appropriately, perhaps, it is believed to have received its first public performance at The Blaengarw Hotel and it became one of the most popular hymns sung during the Religious Revival of 1904. Today it is frequently referred to as the second national anthem of Wales, and features regularly at weddings and funerals, for it speaks of how a pure heart, full of goodness, is more important than riches. That so clearly reflects the unrelenting life of toil and unhappiness that Daniel James experienced, a life which is a representative of thousands of similar lives lived throughout late nineteenth century Wales.

It is also sung with enthusiasm before rugby internationals, too. Personally, I have always found this strange. The music certainly has the power to express the national identity, but any connection between lyrics about pure hearts full of goodness and those who play or watch the game is tenuous to say the least.

Swansea, Sketty
William Thomas 1865

Soothing wrinkles from the brow of agony

The history of Wales has always been tied up with the sea. In the nineteenth century ships drifted in slowly from beyond the horizon bringing trade and ideas, changing lives. The sea was always the route to a new and exciting world, to places of unexpected adventure and danger. And sometimes that danger came to the shore, in the shape of a drunken sailor perhaps, or a fugitive. But once. that danger came as a deadly disease.

Let us start with the grave. Hundreds of people go past along the busy road every day; pupils from the local school might wander along too. But few of them know what is here or realise the warning that this overlooked grave might have for all of us.

Go through the lych gate of St Paul's Church on Sketty Lane in Swansea and you will find it a short distance away, to the left. The ground is uneven and the ivy is pushing slowly into the cracks on the headstone. The grave boundary has disappeared beneath the rough grass. Soon the face and the words upon it will have fallen away in the rain, taking with them their unexpected story. It is important to capture those words which you can still make out, if you look hard enough.

The stone is inscribed on both sides. One side contains the family details.

Sacred to the memory of William, son of William and Margaret Thomas, who died the 29 of September 1865 Aged 25

He weakened my strength in the way: he shortened my days.

The poisoned grave of Sketty

William is buried with his parents and his brother. His days were indeed shortened but in the most unlikely of ways. Because if you look at the other side, you will see why this grave is notable. He died *'of yellow fever, caught while working in Swansea at a yard near where an infected ship, The Hecla from the West Indies was lying.'*

You see, he died in the only recorded outbreak of yellow fever on the mainland of Great Britain. And this decaying gravestone might well be pointing the way to our future.

The Hecla was a modest wooden cargo ship carrying 540 tons of copper ore and 81 tons of copper regulus for the Cobre Mining Company, from Santiago in Cuba. It arrived in the Bristol Channel on Friday 8 September 1865 and picked up a pilot off Lundy Island. The Master reported that he had one very sick man and that he had already lost 3 of his crew during the voyage. The pilot was not aware that they had brought with them something far more important – and deadly - than their copper ore. The ship after all, carried a clean bill of health, and a ship had arrived from Cuba a fortnight earlier with no reported sickness.

The Hecla waited in the Mumbles anchorage overnight and was then towed into Swansea on Saturday 9 September. Men were sent out to support the crew, who were too ill to man the vessel properly. There was a short item in the newspaper too, entitled *'Distressing Shipping News'* about the appearance of *The Hecla* flying a flag at half-mast. People knew what that meant. Death on board.

The crew were paid off and unloading began. Anxious relatives watched as *'one poor fellow (James Saunders), was brought ashore upon a litter and died within a few hours.'* He was immediately buried. The sanitary inspector reported to the mayor the news that he had died, apparently of yellow fever.

Officials realised that they had to isolate those infected, but there was nowhere to receive them. Meetings were urgently called *'to prevent any evil consequences resulting from the impudent steps of bringing a vessel into port when so many of its crew had suffered from so contagious a disease.'* It was obviously a case of negligence. As the *Cambrian* newspaper said a week later, the desire of the ship's captain to be *'free from his plague prison'* and the poor victims to have *'the loving attentions of those gentle nurses whose kindness smoothes wrinkles from the brow of agony'* are perfectly understandable, but their exclusion from port should have been essential. There should have been somewhere where those infected could have been accommodated. *The Hecla* should really have gone to a quarantine station at Milford, set up to deal with *'infectious distempers.'* They knew something was wrong and *'that a fatal disease had been raging on board the vessel her bills of mortality prove.'* But that didn't happen. Presumably they were eager to get home and thought they could get away with it. But once the ship was in the dock it was too late. The disease is transmitted by mosquitoes and they are such small things.

The weather in Swansea was described as having a *'predisposing atmospheric constitution.'* To you and me that means it was hot, of almost *'tropical intensity,'* providing an exciting all-day buffet for insect visitors.

At the time, no one knew how yellow fever was spread. They recognised it as some kind of *'contagion'* and was a consequence of *the 'extraordinary character of the present summer.'* Everything was fine, everything was normal. It was just the weather that had caused it. It was so warm across northern Europe that readers were told that Charles Dickens *'now in Paris has sunstroke. He was insensible for some hours.'*

It was the weather that enabled the insects to survive for long enough to do their work. From 15 September – six days after *The Hecla's* arrival – until 4 October, six days after it was moved from its mooring, twenty people contracted yellow fever, of whom thirteen died. Numerous others suffered less severe symptoms. This still remains the only confirmed outbreak of yellow fever on the English mainland and it was only the return of normal, cooler, weather patterns that prevented it from spreading further.

There was a clear sense of alarm at the appearance of this invisible killer. It was quickly identified as yellow fever. After all, sailors had often died of it before, en route from the West Indies. But it had never before been brought back to shore. There were denials by those who wanted it to be something else, who tried to link it to an outbreak of cattle fever. Yellow fever becoming endemic in Swansea could have a catastrophic effect on trade. So health officials sought desperately to calm the situation, but it is easier to create alarm than it is to allay fears. The press hints at considerable public apprehension. The reality was probably a great deal less measured.

It was imperative to indicate that sanitary arrangements in the town were adequate. A distinguished surgeon, Dr Buchanan from the fever hospital in London, was sent to Swansea. Public meetings were held. Reassurance was necessary. Ironically, they felt that the disease was now somehow in the air around them. They didn't realise that it had wings. The Mayor keen to be seen to be doing something. He announced that the ship, the seamen's clothes and the home of James Saunders had been fumigated. But, as people looked for scapegoats, there were rumours that the Mayor was financially involved in *The Hecla*, accusations which he was forced publicly to deny. That was the real reason, they said, why it had been allowed to dock.

Throughout the press coverage there is an interesting assumption that information should be withheld to prevent public alarm. The details of the symptoms would, we are told, *'be out of place in a newspaper'*, which is not terribly helpful. The authorities knew best, but is hard to accept any circumstances In which such knowledge should be kept secret, even if they did include passing blood and vomiting. It was acknowledged that the people of Swansea were terrified but the *Shipping and Mercantile Gazette* felt all was exaggerated. In 34 days *'there were but 13 deaths in a population of more than 40,000 which cannot be regarded as a severe death rate.'*

And it wasn't only Swansea that was affected. Two of the crew of the *Eleanor* died in Llanelli, more victims of *'this terrible scourge of the tropics'*. Their ship had been alongside *The Hecla* in Swansea docks.

The press was very eager to send out positive messages about how the outbreak was managed, because for a port which relied upon maritime trade, this had the potential to be public relations disaster. Swansea was quickly regarded as an infected port. Spain refused to admit Swansea vessels; other countries imposed restrictions.

Of course, it ended as quickly as it had begun. Once the weather resumed normal service the mosquitoes died and eventually the story faded from view. The death of Lord Palmerstone had much greater national significance. On 3

November 1865 *The Hecla* returned to its trans-Atlantic trade and left Swansea for Valparaiso. Life resumed.

The virus is transmitted by the bite of a mosquito – *aedes aegypti*. The incubation period is usually three to six days, as we can see in the Swansea outbreak. Most cases produce mild flu-like symptoms but if it moves in to a second phase it becomes very nasty indeed. It is called yellow fever because it causes jaundice symptoms, since the virus attacks the liver.

Where death occurs, it is usually the result of multi-organ failure.

There are still over 30,000 deaths every year in unvaccinated populations, largely in tropical and sub-tropical areas. The best means of control lies in controlling the mosquito, which breeds in standing water, just as you would find on a ship like *The Hecla*. The disease was endemic in Cuba at this time. But the link between the disease and insects was not yet established. It was simply caused, they believed, by *'contagion.'*

There was a long article in the *British Medical Journal* about the impossibility of it being yellow fever. They preferred to call it typhoid or some sort of *'Swansea fever.'* Today we are less convinced of our immunity. There have been other examples of tropical diseases striking unexpectedly in the Northern Hemisphere. There was an outbreak of yellow fever in Saint Nazaire in France in 1861 and prior to that in Barcelona, Gibraltar and Lisbon. In 1793 10,000 people died in Philadelphia and there were other outbreaks across America, including New Orleans in 1905.

Malaria was prevalent in Sussex and Kent, with more than 60,000 patients admitted to St Thomas Hospital between 1850 and 1860. Oh yes, germs and viruses can spread across the world – we have seen this ourselves with Covid 19.

Is this our future? Must we come to accept tropical diseases as a consequence of how the world has shrunk or of global warming?

If we eventually become sub-tropical, we will welcome all sorts of diseases transmitted, like yellow fever, by parasites. Tropical killers can travel north. They have before. After all, spiders and snakes in bananas have long been the stuff of legend. But if ever mosquitoes begin to fly again in our sky, then our world will change.

I wonder if we are ready.

Talyllyn, Gwynedd
Jenny Jones, 1884

I will never leave you nor forsake thee

She is buried in the untidy cemetery at the end of the lake, where the water flows out into the Afon Dysynni. Drive along the B4405 and you will find it quite easily. A squat and ancient church, and there, immediately on the right-hand side as you go through the lych gate you will see her, at the top of three stone steps. Nobody knows who erected the stone above her grave. But people have always cared about her.

Facing her Waterloo

Her story has inaccuracies. That is no surprise when you reflect on a long life that goes back long before efficient record keeping. Jenny herself forgot some of the details of her life, since not much of it was written down, but the essentials are real enough.

Here in the churchyard of St. Mary's Church in Talyllyn lies Jenny Jones, a veteran of the Battle of Waterloo. Her story and her longevity were remembered for a while in popular horse brasses, in commemorative china bells and figurines. But the world soon moved on. Now she is a collectable, an antique in a window. But it is such a story.

She was born Jane Drumble in Ireland, though no one is quite sure when. It is recorded on the grave in St. Mary's as 1789, although the census records suggest a more probable date of 1797. Whatever date you chose, she lived a long and eventful life, spanning almost the whole of the nineteenth century, which is quite an achievement. The inscription that indicates that she was born in Scotland is probably inaccurate, but there can be no doubt about the key moment in her life – and that was when she met Lewis Griffith.

Napoleon played his part, of course, as he often did, and perhaps she was always grateful for that. You see, conscription was necessary to form an army to confront him and the parish of Talyllyn in North Wales was obliged to provide one man for the Militia. A ballot was held and immediately the winner broke down in tears. He had indeed 'drawn the short straw'. Help was at hand in the shape of a young local farm worker, Lewis Griffith, who agreed to enlist in his place. For him this was an adventure. An unrivalled opportunity to see the world beyond those dark wet hills.

He was posted first to far away Wrexham and then on to Dublin for training. There, one Sunday morning on Church Parade in Granard, Lewis saw Jane. In later years she couldn't remember how old she was, except that she was very young. It probably happened in 1811, when she was 14. Jane was an educated town girl from a wealthy family; he was an illiterate farmer's boy from Wales. Soon they began to see each other secretly. They might have been young but were both convinced by their love.

When Lewis was due to leave Ireland, he vowed that they would not be separated. The colonel gave him permission to marry, with the banns called twice in one day to expedite matters. They were married in Granard and she was immediately ostracised by her family for it. Now all she had was Lewis, and so she followed him.

It is likely that she became a camp follower and accompanied her husband to war, perhaps tending the wounded and washing uniforms. What we do know, is that he joined the 23rd Royal Welch Fusiliers on 6 April 1814, when he gave his age as 19. Then, when the regiment turned up in Ostend in 1815, Jane was with them, with her six-month-old daughter and she was part of the march that took the troops to the Battle of Waterloo on 18 June 1815.

Understandably, preparations to feed the army were incomplete and they foraged for what they could, killing farm animals across Belgium, but what little Jane could find was stolen from her in the camp. It was a hard march.

On the morning of the battle, she marched on to the field with Lewis, to the section of the battle known as Hougoumont, where the Fusiliers were ordered to clear the French Imperial Guard from the field. She stayed with him whilst he loaded his gun. He was in the front rank and, at the point at which he was commanded to kneel in order to fire the first volley, Jane was ordered to return to camp and take her baby out of immediate danger. Even then, health and safety was really tiresome. As she retired, a French volley filled the air, narrowly missing her.

Jane took refuge in a chapel which was soon destroyed by

cannon fire that killed many sheltering there. After that, things got a little confusing.

Jane was not the only woman on the field that day. When the bodies were buried, there were many female corpses. The two opposing armies were communities on the move and they brought with them many members.

French regiments were accompanied by women called *cantinieres* or *vivandieres* who wore a type of uniform. Their job was to sell tobacco and brandy to the troops and to care for the wounded. In the British army normally only about 6 soldiers in each company were permitted to take their wives on active service, but those who were there acquired similar duties to the French. It was inevitable that they should become casualties themselves in the chaos of the battle. A cannon shell killed the wife of a sergeant of the 28th Foot as she carried her injured husband from the field. Another woman was found dead, with her child by her side.

There were happier stories amongst the carnage. Private Peter McMullen of the 27th Foot was seriously wounded and, as his wife carried him out of battle, she was hit by a musket ball that fractured her leg. They were both taken to hospital in Antwerp where she was safely delivered of a baby girl. She was christened Frederica McMullen Waterloo. Martha Deacon walked back to Brussels in the pouring rain, dressed only in a black silk dress, together with her children, looking for her husband. There she found him safe and promptly gave birth to a baby girl who was christened Waterloo Deacon. Margaret Tolmie found her husband still alive in a pile of bodies ready for burial. She too gave birth to a baby girl the next day.

There must have been something in the water. Mind you, there do seem to have been girls everywhere. One of the last surviving witnesses of the battle died in 1903, aged 92. Barbara Moon had been the 4-year-old daughter of a colour sergeant and had ridden in a cart across Waterloo as her mother searched for her husband.

For many of the camp followers however, the victory was followed by the awful process of picking over the remains of battle. The battle itself may have lasted the whole of a day, but the aftermath went on for much longer. Women would carefully pick through the twisted piles of bodies for traces of their husbands. Some would be found wounded; others dead and horribly mutilated; others not found at all. It must have been an awful place to be. The blood, the vermin, the smell. The women competed with looters of both sexes, who would cut off fingers, even from the living, to steal their rings. For them this vast sea of bodies was merely an opportunity. Never forget about Waterloo teeth. These were taken from the dead on the battlefield, formed into dentures, and sold to the toothless for years afterwards.

Even after the corpses had been cleared, bereaved women still wandered the field, sometimes in a state of increasing hysteria, as they came to terms with awful reality. And soon, for many of them there were no more straws at which to clutch.

In such an atmosphere, Jane spent three days looking for Lewis. He had not answered to his name in the roll call on 19 June, the day after the battle. She would have known at this time that the regiment had suffered many casualties. In fact they had lost 10 officers and 89 men, either killed or wounded. She must have feared the worst, though the absence of a body must have been of some comfort. Eventually, she was told that he had already been taken to Brussels for treatment. There she searched for two days without success. But on the third day, Lewis was eventually found in the Elizabeth Hospital, where seven pieces of shrapnel had been extracted from his shoulder.

Remember what it says on her gravestone, and then realise who was speaking those words. *"I will never leave you nor forsake thee."*

They stayed in Brussels for a month whilst he recuperated and then he re-joined the Regiment. All the Fusiliers received a medal and an additional payment of £2. 11. 4d for the defeat of the Imperial Guard. Lewis' medal was later stolen.

Lewis saw out his seven years in the army, with Jane continuing to act as laundry maid, nurse and, of course, mother until April 1821. He was not entitled to a pension, receiving instead £5 blood money for his wound.

With their service over, they returned to Lewis' home. Where else could they go? Her family had disowned her. So they settled at Talyllyn, and Lewis went to work in the slate quarries in Corris. All that drama and excitement of war was replaced by a hard life of unrelenting physical labour. But perhaps it was preferable to the dangers of shrapnel. Here in this tiny place, The End of the Lake, they made their home. The low grey scattered houses formed their community. The huge dark hills their horizons.

Then, in 1837, Lewis was killed by a rock fall. The love of her life was gone. What the French Imperial Guard couldn't achieve was accomplished very simply in the grim rocks of Corris.

But a harsh economic reality dominated the lives of our ancestors. She had once married for love; now she needed to marry for survival. This time, Jane married John Jones of Talyllyn. She worked when she could, washing the laundry for the local hotels, just as she had done for the regiment. She may also have worked as a schoolteacher, or more likely as an assistant, at the Maes Pandy School in Abergynolwyn. But the longer she lived, the less capable she was for work. John Jones died and Jenny was then maintained by the parish of Dolgellau at a rate of 5 shillings a week. She lived out her life in this tiny place by the clear waters, amongst the dark hills.

Jane – or Jenny as she became known – had lived through exciting times with the man whom she loved. Waterloo was a tumultuous day, truly a turning point in history. A close-run thing, as Wellington described it. And Jenny was there. The boundaries of her life may have subsequently reduced to those of a low slate cottage in Snowdonia but she had been part of it. In a time and a place where many of her neighbours would struggle to speak English, she could converse in French. Nothing could ever change that.

Census records are often inaccurate and as you track through the details recorded at ten-year intervals, hers contain inconsistencies. Whilst her grave may suggest that she was 95, a more accurate figure is probably 87. It is still, nonetheless, a remarkable age, lived when life could be so harsh. She died on 11 April 1884 and was buried 4 days later. It was by John Jones' name that she was known by others. It is this surname that appears on her grave. But it was as Lewis that she knew herself.

In the 1881 census she is described as handicapped and blind, and perhaps, thus shut away from daily reality in her own world, she was once again back with Lewis, the man who had changed her life.

Tenby, Pembrokeshire
Robert Recorde 1558

Zenzizenzizenic

You know about Robert Recorde's invention. Of course you do. Everyone does. You have used it, perhaps even on a daily basis. It is just that no one has told you it was him. But it was.

This story begins in St Mary's Church in Tenby. It is a very attractive place in the heart of the walled town, a place of memorials and the perfect place for a wander. Inside there is an excellent classically-inspired sculpture to Captain Bird Allen who died in 1841 on an expedition to help suppress the slave trade in Africa. He wrote in a letter home that *'it has pleased the Almighty to lay his hand upon us with the chastisement of sickness.'* His memorial puts it more succinctly though, when it says that he fell victim *'to the climate of the river Niger.'* You can also see one of my favourite memorial tablets in the whole of Wales, the one to Peggy Davies. It had been written with considerable affection for a woman who, for 42 years, had attended visiting ladies who came to Tenby for fashionable sea-bathing. On 29 September 1809 *'in the water she was seized with apoplexy and expired, aged 82.'*

Interesting though these stories are, neither of them is the reason why we are looking at St Mary's. There is another notable memorial, that to the remarkable Robert Recorde. He was born in Tenby, probably in 1510, and is perhaps the greatest of all Welsh scholars, for he was the man who drew two short parallel lines and so invented the equals sign. Recorde = immortality.

There are no pictures of him, which is a shame because Robert Recorde has touched the lives of everyone, even if they don't

178

realise it. There is this memorial of course in the church, but the only existing picture of him, on which the carving in the church is modelled, is probably not a likeness of him at all.

IN MEMORY OF
ROBERT RECORDE,
THE EMINENT MATHEMATICIAN,
WHO WAS BORN AT TENBY, circa 1510.
TO HIS GENIUS WE OWE THE EARLIEST
IMPORTANT ENGLISH TREATISES ON
ALGEBRA, ARITHMETIC, ASTRONOMY, and GEOMETRY:
HE ALSO INVENTED THE SIGN OF
EQUALITY = NOW UNIVERSALLY ADOPTED
BY THE CIVILIZED WORLD.

ROBERT RECORDE
WAS COURT PHYSICIAN TO
KING EDWARD VI. and QUEEN MARY.
HE DIED IN LONDON,
1558.

The memorial adds to the dignity of the church, rather than subtracting from it.

He was born such a long time ago that much of his life equals a mystery and there is a great deal that we don't know. I can tell you that his father Thomas was Lord Mayor of Tenby and that Robert was destined for an academic career. He went to Oxford University, possibly to study medicine and graduated in 1531. He was certainly a highly educated man with a wide range of interests, which included Anglo-Saxon language and history. He seems to have been a teacher of mathematics and to have spent some time at Cambridge University too, where he was recognised as a Doctor of Medicine, an area of knowledge which included astrology and cosmology. I suspect that my own GP skipped those lectures, which occasionally acts as a barrier to imaginative diagnosis, I find. Nevertheless, I can confirm that Recorde soon moved to London to practise medicine.

In 1547 Henry VIII died and was succeeded by ten-year old Edward VI. In the same year Recorde's work *The Urinal of Physick* was published, an essential text that explored how you could diagnose illness from the condition of a patient's urine. It established him as a prominent medical figure. We can see this because he was asked to assess the mental condition of someone imprisoned in the Tower of London who had been charged with being a false prophet. He probably went on to practise as a physician in Edward's court and he had certainly established himself there by 1549, when he moved into the Civil Service, becoming Controller of the Royal Mint in Bristol and of the new London mint on the Strand. He was responsible for the introduction of the first silver crown to have the date in Arabic rather than Roman numerals.

But this was not a job without its dangers. The previous incumbent in Bristol had been sent to the Tower, and whilst Recorde was a highly intelligent man, his skills did not equip him for the uncertainty of the times in which he lived. He got himself into particular difficulties with Sir William Herbert who was an influential figure and a governor of the young King Edward. He was active in suppressing unrest in parts of the country and requested money to fund his army to carry that out. Recorde however refused, since the request did not come from the King. In response, Herbert closed the Bristol mint and Recorde was placed under house arrest for sixty days. He had made himself a dangerous enemy.

He was sufficiently rehabilitated by 1551 when he was appointed as Controller of Mines and Money in Ireland, with responsibility for the silver mines in Wexford and the Dublin mint. Recorde was a loyal protestant but when the regime changed in 1553 with Queen Mary's accession, Herbert was rewarded for his loyal support of the new Catholic Queen with the title of Earl of Pembroke and with a position as a Privy councillor. Recorde immediately found himself on the wrong side of a significant political divide.

They clashed again in a dispute about mining in Wexford and smelting rights at Pentyrch, near Cardiff, and Pembroke recalled Recorde from Ireland. This was devious Tudor politics, nothing more than that, but Robert Recorde became one of its victims. He foolishly accused Pembroke of misconduct, which proved to be a significant mistake.

In response, Pembroke sued Recorde for libel in October 1556. Robert Recorde was out of his depth and was told to pay £1000 in damages which was exactly the amount he was owed for his work in Ireland, but which hadn't been paid. He did not have sufficient money and was then imprisoned in Southwark, where he died in 1558. His Will included small legacies for nine children – each one of them a record holder in their own way. Ironically in 1570 his estate was finally awarded that £1000 – twelve years after his death.

It is for his maths that we remember him today, including his book *The Pathway to Knowledge* from 1551 which is about geometry. If I am honest, it would be fair to say that for me geometry has never been anything other than an over-grown, barely-trodden track leading absolutely nowhere, but Robert Recorde clearly felt rather differently. He also wrote *The Castle of Knowledge* about astronomy and *The Treasure of Knowledge*. He clearly had no time for modest titles.

His books are generally in the form of a dialogue between

master and servant. Now, I have read extracts from them and all I can say is that if I had been the servant, then Mr Recorde would have had to speak a great deal more slowly. The important thing though, is that these books were not written in Latin but in English and were intended to be simple and accessible for ordinary people, the same principles which underpinned the earliest book on childcare in English, written by Thomas Phaer in 1545, who features in this book in the Cilgerran section.

The title of his volume, *The Whetstone of Witte* from 1557, suggests that it is a book by which you can sharpen your mathematical understanding and through it he established his lasting fame. It is a teaching manual for an advanced mathematical course, in which he introduced the plus and minus signs already in use in Germany, but his greatest success was the equals sign. Recorde got fed up with writing 'is equal to' and designed the new symbol because, as he said, he could think of nothing more equal than two parallel lines of the same length. I imagine you cannot either.

Recorde invented some other English mathematical terms which I am disappointed to say did not catch on – like '*cinkangle*' for pentagon, and '*siseangle*' for hexagon. But I think his triumph was the invention of a term which sounds like the name of a green-skinned galactic tyrant in a cheap 1950's science fiction film. He described a number raised to the eighth power as a '*zenzizenzizenic*' and went on to explain that *it doth represent the square of squares squaredly*. I couldn't put it better myself.

Robert Recorde = Tenby's son = Tenby's pride

Trawsfynydd, Gwynedd

Ellis Evans (Hedd Wyn), 1917
Buried in Artillery Wood Cemetery, Boezinge, Belgium

White and Black

This grave takes us to Belgium and the site of the Third Battle of Ypres in 1917. But it is a journey that begins on the hills of North Wales above Trawsfynydd. For this is the story of the Black Bard.

We visited his grave on a cold February afternoon in Artillery Wood Cemetery at Boezinge, just outside Ypres. As always, we could see a mass of white headstones, each an individual life extinguished too soon and the occasional poppy left by a relative who can now never have met the fallen. So many lives. It wasn't only the biting wind that made our eyes water.

But one grave stands out, for it is more acknowledged than the rest. And the grave register by the gate is also full of children's projects and tributes.

In Artillery Wood Cemetery, Boezinge

For this is the grave of Private Ellis Humphrey Evans, 61117, Royal Welch Fusiliers, the great Welsh poet. He became known as The Black Bard. But to begin with he was known as Hedd Wyn. White Peace.

He was born in January 1887 at Penlan in Trawsfynydd and he spent his childhood on the family farm, Yr Ysgwrn. He left school at 14 and worked as a shepherd but was determined to continue with his education. He would walk to Bala to borrow books from the library and he would spend his days on the hills writing poetry. His bardic name of Hedd Wyn was awarded at a local poetry festival.

He did work as a miner in the South Wales coalfields for a while, but he realised that his vocation was out on the hills, writing poetry. His reputation grew and he won his first bardic chair at Bala in 1907, followed by others at Eisteddfodau at Llanuwchllyn, Pwllheli and Pontardawe. It was his ambition to win the National, and in fact he came second at Aberystwyth in 1916. Always, his bardic name was Hedd Wyn.

Evans never embraced the idea the war. He was a pacifist. Here are the first two lines of his poem 'Rhyfel' (War.)

Gwae fi fy myn mewn oes mor ddreng

A Duw ar drai ar orwel pell

(Woe is my life in such a bitter age, / As God fades on the horizon's canopy.)

There is no sense of glory or triumph here. Only the thought that God had turned his back on man.

He had no desire to join the army and was protected initially by his occupation. Some farm workers were exempt, on the basis that theirs was a vital occupation.

But even in the hills the war scarred families, their sons never to return home. His contemporaries were dying and he was writing

184

poems in their memory and working on the farm. However as casualties mounted, the rules were changed and Ellis Evans' fate was sealed. The army needed more men and there was not enough work at Yr Ysgwrn to keep all the Evans boys at home. Someone had to go.

In order to spare his more enthusiastic younger brother, he joined the Royal Welch Fusiliers in February 1917 as a private. From Wrexham Barracks the new recruits were sent to Liverpool but cut unconvincing military figures. Coming down from their farms they would have seemed like foreigners, reluctant to speak English and all at sea in an alien world. Soldiers they were not. It was said of Ellis, *'He was a silent fellow. It would appear he could speak but little English, or if he could, he did not.'* The army represented a world he did not wish to join. He was only there out of duty and he was more concerned to complete his poem *Yr Arwr* (The Hero) in time for the National Eisteddfod in September.

It was to be held in Birkenhead. Outside Wales of course, but home to many Welsh people working in the city, either in essential war industries or teaching and nursing.

His chance to refine his poem came when he was sent home after basic training for seven weeks. This was the last time he would see his family and his home.

Private Ellis Evans, of the 15th Bn. Royal Welch Fusiliers, was despatched on active service to Flanders on 9 June 1917. It was a grim place. He wrote in a letter home, *'Heavy weather, heavy soul, heavy heart.'* There was, he said, *'a curse upon the land.'* He wrote in his poem 'Y Blotyn Du.'

> *We have no right to anything*
>
> *But the old and withered earth*
>
> *That is all in chaos.*

The rhythm and the certainties of the seasons that he knew so well, and that he had just left, were replaced by mud and blood.

Ellis Evans' statue in Trawsfynydd

The poem was submitted just in time, sent from France on 15 July 1917. It describes the realities of war for both the soldiers and their families at home. It escaped censorship by the army since, naturally, it was written in Welsh. All the subalterns who checked it were English.

It was his misfortune that the 15th Battalion of the Royal Welch Fusiliers was part of the 38th Division, which had been selected to lead the assault on Pilckem Ridge. This would be the Third Battle of Ypres, also known as Passchendaele. The division was regarded as having under-performed in the action at Mametz Wood in the Battle of the Somme. This therefore was a chance for them to redeem themselves.

They practised their role on a replica of the German trenches built behind the front line in France during June and they were moved up for the attack on 30 July. In the assault, the 15th Battalion were required to attack a regimental headquarters and a telephone exchange. They succeeded in this objective, but every officer in the battalion was killed. So was Evans. General Haig described it as *'a fine day's work.'* 31,000 soldiers were casualties on that fine day.

A plaque made of Welsh slate on a brick wall at the Hagebos crossroad now marks the place where the wounded Evans was taken on 31 July 1917. The first aid post received him with chest wounds from shrapnel. He died 4 days later. Although his first language was Welsh, his last words are said to have been English. *'I am very happy.'* And so he died, so far away from the hills of north Wales. In their peace and solitude he had reflected and written. In the noise and chaos of Flanders he died, like so many others.

Back in Liverpool a group of refugees from the Belgian town of Mechelen were given warm hospitality. One of them was Eugene Van Fleteren, who made reproduction furniture. In an act of gratitude for the help he had received, he made the traditional carved chair for the National Eisteddfod. It was to be awarded on Thursday 6 September 1917. A Flanders chair for a Flanders casualty.

As a day of celebration, it was not a success. Of the two choirs from the Royal Welch Fusiliers who had sung to such acclaim two years earlier, only the conductor had survived and he was badly injured. And when Archdruid Dyfed announced the winner of the bardic chair, for his work *Yr Arwr*, there was no reply in acceptance, for Hedd Wyn had died six weeks earlier.

'Instead of the usual chairing ceremony the chair was draped in a black pall amidst death-like silence and the bards came forward in long procession to place their muse- tribute of englyn or couplet on the draped chair in memory of the dead bard hero.' (The Western Mail.)

Hedd Wyn. The Black Bard.

After the ceremony the chair was taken away by train and cart to the family farm, to a room set aside in his memory.

At the end of the war Hedd Wyn's poems were published as *'Cerdi'r Bugail'* (Shepherd's Songs) and a statue was erected in Trawsfynydd, not as a soldier but as a shepherd, which is probably how he would have liked to be remembered. It was unveiled by his mother in 1923. A petition to the Commonwealth War Graves Commission was granted so that his grave in Artillery Wood does not read simply as E.H. Ellis but Y Prifardd Hedd Wyn, meaning Principal Bard, Hedd Wyn.

On Welsh slate at the Hagebos Crossroads

He has not been forgotten. His old school in Trawsfynydd is

now called Ysgol Hedd Wyn in his honour and school projects take children to his graveside. A Welsh -language film of his life was nominated for an Oscar in 1992 and in the same year, on the 75th anniversary of his death, a joint venture between the people of Trawsfynydd and Ypres produced that slate plaque on a wall at Hagebos crossroads. In Welsh, English and Flemish it is a fine Welsh slate on fine Flanders brick. Made to last, like memories.

At the base of Ellis Evan's statue in Trawsfynydd there is a tribute he wrote for a friend killed earlier in the war. He could have written this about himself.

> *His sacrifice will not be forgotten*
>
> *His face so dear will ever be remembered*
>
> *Though Germany's iron fist by his blood was stained.*

Every November our thoughts turn to the past, to the awful destruction of a generation. The world would never be the same again. We should never forget what happened and what the world lost. All that potential, all those possibilities, wiped out. Forever.

And amongst all the other things we lost, Wales lost a great poet.

Tredegar, Blaenau Gwent
Cefn Golau 1832

The Cholera Cemetery

It is an astonishing sight. Apparently abandoned gravestones on an exposed moorland, well away from the cemetery where you would otherwise expect to find them. Forlorn, as if they have been dropped randomly from the sky to impale the soft boggy hill top. It was for scenes like this that the word 'bleak' was invented.

The abandoned graves that once induced terror

This is Cefn Golau. The Hill of Light between Tredegar and Rhymney. This is the cholera cemetery. It is quite remarkable. Indeed there are few more moving sights in Wales than this collection of broken stones. They speak of a horrible, cruel and painful death that arrived seemingly at random and without warning.

Cholera, the King of Terrors. Silent. Unexpected. Vicious. Indiscriminate.

These stones are heavily weathered now, the inscriptions flaking away and crumbling into the rough grass. Once there were markers for over 230 victims. Now only 26 stones remain, surrounded by broken shards and fragments.

Cholera was the scourge of the valleys in the nineteenth century. The terrible conditions in which people lived and worked provided the perfect breeding ground for this virulent strain that came originally from the East. Vibrio cholerae. Asiatic cholera.

It causes profuse watery diarrhoea (called 'rice water stools') and violent vomiting leading rapidly to collapse. '*Shrivelling of the skin, suppression of urine*' and complete dehydration. Death could occur very quickly.

The essentials of life – food and water – had been contaminated. These essentials were the killers. And the poor had nowhere to hide.

It was a constant threat. Serious outbreaks would strike fear into the heart of the community. You can't see it but it can kill you. And quickly. This was the most horrifying aspect of the epidemic. Families could be fit and healthy in the morning and dead by sunset. It respected no one.

The cholera cemetery at Cefn Golau remembers two major epidemics in Tredegar. The first in 1832 and the second in 1849. The dates, where they can be read, are from August and September when the infection was at its most virulent. There are occasionally dates outside of the great epidemics on the stones, but these indicate that survivors chose to be buried with those that they loved, even though the cemetery was abandoned by the locals through fear of infection. For a long time, it was believed that cholera was the *'result of odours, emanations and miasmas from the earth.'* So best bury the bodies well away from anyone.

The cemetery was started in 1832 when a circular declared that all graveyards should be closed to cholera victims in an attempt at infection control. An alternative site was needed high on the mountain, well away from homes. A similar cemetery was established near Merthyr at Pant coed Ifor, but that appears to be lost. All we have now is this cemetery above Tredegar. Welcome to Cefn Golau.

Cholera came back in 1849 and its inexorable progress was tracked in newspaper reports. In June 1849 it is in Merthyr and Cardiff. Ten deaths from cholera are announced in Cardiff alone on 22 June. A week later it is Aberavon and Neath. Robert Leyshon the mayor of Neath dies. The good people of Swansea are congratulating themselves on their fine standards of hygiene in July. Soon 262 people were dead.

Then in August an excise man called Price, who lived in Charles Street, became the first victim in Tredegar. By the end of the month almost every street in the town was affected. Lime and disinfectants were distributed, all manner of cures were tried. They covered themselves in ointments; they took brandy; they inhaled camphor. A Doctor Wilkins advised the use of *'copper smoke'* as a preventative. But to little avail.

The chapels were packed as people sought salvation in religion. They began to leave their homes and move into the countryside. Those who stayed behind avoided funerals to the extent that there were not enough to assist in burying the dead. Families were forced to bury their own dead in the middle of the night on the mountain. The lonely and eerie cemetery of Cefn Golau continued to grow.

There was an additional fear too. Victims were buried so quickly that the illness carried with it the additional terror of being buried alive. In Swansea doctors were accused of prescribing such excessive amounts of sedation to patients that it was killing them.

Some had an idea of the causes of the disease but many had no clue at all. The disease appeared to establish itself in trading ports and then spread quickly inland into the areas of high population where poor housing and malnutrition allowed the disease to thrive. It is no surprise that it was considered to be an unfortunate catastrophe visited upon the lives of the poor.

In May 1849 twenty-four people died of cholera near the Glamorganshire Canal in Cardiff. A local doctor, John Sutherland, reported that *'the end of the canal nearest the sea was emptied in order to admit repairs of the lock. By this process a large surface of black putrescent mud was exposed to the direct action of the hot sun, and the result was that very offensive effluvia were immediately perceptible.'*

Sutherland had no doubt in his mind about the origins of the disease. Smells and mud. Yet the real cause was staring everyone in the face.

Look at what happened in Swansea gaol. A prisoner died and the premises were washed out by a *'water engine worked by the policemen of the borough. Three days later, David Jones, one of the policemen employed, died an acute death from the disease.'* The evidence to point the finger at dirty water was there, it just hadn't been recognised.

Huge numbers of people lived in filthy conditions. Small back-to-back hovels, continually damp, with no toilets and no access to clean water – it was a nightmare waiting to happen. Buckets of soiled water were emptied into the street and the foul contents would flow back into the houses whenever it rained, or seep into the wells where they collected their water. Drinking water contaminated with faeces? It doesn't bear thinking about.

It is astonishing to think that it took people such a long time to work out what was the cause. The Cambrian newspaper reflected wisely that *'The greatest number of cases presented themselves on Sunday and*

Monday…and we fear it is with much truth that the cause is to be attributed to the excesses of the preceding evenings.' It was so much easier to blame the excesses of the poor, than to consider that the epidemics had a different origin that might require responsible action.

And even when responsible action was taken, it was not always well received. Sixteen years later, in Dowlais in 1865, a typhoid outbreak was quickly followed by the arrival of cholera and the ironworks there opened a temporary hospital to deal with cases. The gathering together of cholera victims in order to facilitate more efficient treatment was extremely unpopular. Workers rioted and broke into the hospital where they threatened and insulted the nurses. They threatened to strike if the hospital continued and the company felt they had no alternative other than to close the facility completely. A triumph for fear and ignorance.

Tredegar was merely one place amongst many in Wales that was ravaged by cholera. Wrexham, where *'stagnant filth meets the eye in every bypath and in places of public resort,'* Flint, Northop, Halkyn. In Welshpool the disease ravaged the crowded slums of Powell's Row. Soon it was in Newtown.

In Holyhead the only place the authorities could find to accommodate the sick was a lodging house owned by Caddy Owen. It was the place where they used to send young orphan girls. It was also a well-known brothel. It is not surprising that few had any confidence in the ability of Holyhead's authorities to deal with the outbreak. Caernarvon couldn't cope either. A Dr Seaton was sent from London to advise the local authority. He reported that Caernarvon was an *'abominable sink of disease.'*

In the south, the Industrial Revolution had not bothered to develop any sanitary infrastructure along with the factories and the mines. Most of the valley towns appear to have been wallowing in an unsanitary soup of diarrhoea and vermin. The streets were described as *'complete networks of filth.'* An official report said of Merthyr that *'Death is always busy here.'* The only advice that the population could be given was to practise moderation. You might want to try '*The Celebrated Cambrian Medicine for Cholera, Typhus and Worms*', '*Spirits of Camphor*' or indeed '*Humphrey's Indian Remedy*' from Aberystwyth. But the best available advice was to trust in God.

The cholera epidemics had two major long-term effects. In the first place it gave a huge boost to church and chapel attendance. There are stories of chapels that were full of worshippers at 5 o'clock in the morning, for the disease was clearly visited upon the ungodly. The death of Rev. J.T. Davies, Baptist minister of Blaenavon on 31 August 1849, was obviously an oversight.

Secondly, and perhaps more importantly, it stimulated the enormous improvements in public health in the second part of the century. This would have been of little solace to the poor of Tredegar, who were ostracised even in death. Just ordinary people, selected to suffer a cruel death seemingly at random.

In the Library museum there is the first gravestone that was erected at Cefn Golau. The inscription reads

William Thomas Wheelwright late of Swansea
Who departed this life at Tredegar Iron Works, October 21st
1832, aged 38 years.
He was the first to die of the cholera and was interred in this burial
ground.
This stone was placed at the expense of his friends at the Tredegar
Iron Works.

Many of the remaining stones in Cefn Golau have fallen over. Exposed. Neglected. So weathered as to be unreadable. But the others still lean despite the attention of the ponies, a reminder to a world that seems to have forgotten them. Their only companions now are the ponies and the sheep that graze and the dark black crows that watched us closely from the few wind-blasted trees.

195

Cefn Golau cemetery is divided by the B4256 road between Tredegar and Rhymney. If you are driving up the hill from Tredegar you will find a small mountain road on the left-hand side, just before the cemetery. It is signposted to Abertysswg. Drive a short distance along the road and over a cattle grid. You will see a large lay by or parking area on your right-hand side, by the side of a large natural pond. You can see the cholera cemetery a short distance away on the same side of the road to the left of the pond.

You cannot fail to be moved by what you see there. I have never been anywhere quite like Cefn Golau.

Cefn Golau

Tresaith, Ceredigion
Allen Raine 1906

The Dearest Spot on Earth.

She is a sadly neglected figure today and yet towards the end of her life she was one of the best-selling authors in the world, selling over two million copies of her novels, all of which are set in Cardiganshire. And that is where Allen Raine is buried, in one of the most beautiful places you can imagine, in St Michael's Church, Penbryn, close to her home in Tresaith. She was laid to rest in the old circular churchyard next to her husband who had died two years earlier. This was where they had married more than thirty years earlier. One of the floral tributes was sent by a sailor called Rees Thomas, and included a quotation from her novel, *Torn Sails*.

Torn sails and broken mast, but the boat is safe at home at last.

Allen Raine, resting in Tresaith

The polished oak coffin, was simply inscribed '*Anne Adaliza Puddicombe. Died June 21st 1908; aged 71 years* and the mourners *were greatly touched by the realisation of what pain the deceased had unflinchingly borne.*' As the local paper went on to say, '*Her death was a peaceful one, although necessarily painful in the extreme, but she bore it with fortitude.*'

Raine was born as Anne Adaliza Evans on 6 October 1836 in Bank House on Bridge Street in Newcastle Emlyn, the eldest child of Benjamin Evans, a solicitor. She was educated privately, initially in Cheltenham by Mrs Solly, in a cultured and literary household - her husband knew Dickens and George Eliot was a regular visitor. Ada soon moved to London but every summer of her childhood was spent in the seaside village of Tresaith. Her affection for the place never deserted her - all her books are inspired by Tresaith and Llangrannog. It was, she said, '*the dearest spot on earth.*' She was musical and artistic, a keen botanist and fluent in both English and Welsh. For a while she lived in suburban London and then returned to Newcastle Emlyn in 1856. Little is known of her life until her marriage to Beynon Puddicombe, a banker and the son of a solicitor from London in April 1872.

'*All who know the estimable qualities of the bride and bridegroom, which have endeared them to a numerous circle of friends and acquaintances, must join in the sincerest wishes for their future welfare and happiness, and in the hope that their union may be attended with all the blessings this earthly life can afford, accompanied with as little as may be of its sorrows.*'

Sadly it didn't work out like that.

After a honeymoon in Devon, they settled in Addiscombe near Croydon, but for at least ten years (some say as many as fifteen) after her marriage, she was virtually bedridden, kept a prisoner, they said, on her sofa. Once she had recovered, her husband—a banking executive who excelled as an amateur painter - had some kind of mental health crisis which left him paralysed. It was now time for Ada to repay the care and devotion he had given her. They moved to Tresaith in 1900, to a gabled bungalow called Bronmor built for Beynon Puddicombe with his generous pension.

Ada came to her writing later in life. She had had a troubled time of things, after all. At one time she had been a frequent contributor to a local magazine called *Home Sunshine*, but in 1894 she submitted *Ynysoer* a story dealing with a fishing community on a fictional island off the Cardiganshire coast, for the National Eisteddfod in Caernarfon. She shared the first prize and the book was serialised in the North Wales Observer, although only published posthumously, as *Where Billows Roll*.

She struggled to find anyone to accept her next work, *Mifanwy*. It was rejected by six different publishers; books set in Wales were no more popular then than they are today. The book was eventually accepted by Hutchinson, with a new title *A Welsh Singer*, after she paid them £20 to read her manuscript. It certainly was money well spent; on its publication in 1897 it became an instant success.

Allen Raine wrote every afternoon from two to four, lying on her sofa and dictating her story to an amanuensis. The rest of her day was devoted to her husband. She was a rapid and prolific writer. *Torn Sail*, published in 1898, was a triumph and in almost every following year, a new work appeared - *By Berwen Banks* in 1899, *Garthowen* in 1900 and *A Welsh Witch*, her most complex work, was published in 1902. *On the Wings of the Wind* which appeared in 1903 was well received by Spectator Magazine, though they thought the book was written by a man. *Neither Storehouse nor Barn*, appearing first in serial form in the Cardiff Times, was another title published posthumously.

Although she wrote in English, her knowledge of Welsh comes through in her sympathetic understanding of her characters. During her life she formed a very intimate relationship with rural life in Wales and was always able to find romance and poetry within it. When a journalist asked her why she often presented an idealised picture of her characters, she admitted that there were unpleasant people in all walks of life but she did not consider it necessary to *wade through the mud lying underneath the stream when there were so many flowers growing on its banks.*

Raine is sentimental sometimes, but her writing is always based on what she saw around her. She was writing about her own people. As she said towards the end of her life, she was happy that she would always be able to say that she had never written in her books anything about which she needed to be ashamed. She went on, *'there (is) scarcely one scene depicted in my books which I have not personally witnessed or at least known to have occurred.'* Consequently, what she writes is a wonderful window into the disappeared world our rural past. Her books satisfy a yearning for a less complicated and perhaps more picturesque life, where boy meets girl, they part, and after much trauma they are finally re-united. It is a comforting world of moral certainties, where good and love always triumph. If you want to try her work, and I certainly recommend it, you might like to start with *A Life's Chase*, a short story which captures very well the boredom of agricultural life. The arrival of a tramp, *ever haunted by some mysterious dread,* and the casual cruelty he receives, provides a moment of entertainment.

Her work also played a vital part in the development of early Welsh Cinema – at least three of her books were turned into silent films that were shot on location in the area, in which local villagers were used as extras. *The Welsh Singer,* featuring Florence Turner (*'in her latest and greatest triumph'*) was filmed *'among the wild glens and rugged mountains of Wales'* which, according to the Cardiff press, ensured that *'the finest characteristics of the children of Wales are shown at their best.'* Sadly, all the film versions of her work have been lost. When they went, something precious disappeared. Photographs taken during production are all that remain of films that were once so very popular in Wales.

And that pseudonym? It has been observed that she once translated into English a poem sequence by the bard Ceiriog, the leading characters of which were Alun Mabon and Menna Rhen and that she merely combined the names. She explained it herself, with a little more drama, when she said that one night, she dreamt she saw the words '*Allen Raine*' in large white letters on the wall of her bedroom. In the morning her husband, on hearing of her dream, advised her to adopt the name.

Beynon Puddicombe died in 1906, shortly before Ada developed breast cancer which her consultant, rather fancifully I think, said was probably induced by trouble and grief. '*Brave to the last, for two years Mrs. Puddicombe endured the always increasing sufferings, her straight, slight figure and brown hair scarcely touched with grey, giving as little idea of the torments so uncomplainingly borne as of her real age.*'

Despite her fame she was regarded as modest, unassuming and kind by the local people. *The* Carmarthen Weekly Reporter said she '*was merciful of all human failing and charitable to the verge of indiscretion, having only quite recently virtually adopted a peasant's boy who had been treated unkindly*'.

In the days before she died, Ada wrote a touching verse in the autograph book of Miss Thomas, the nurse who had been looking after her.

> *Oh maiden with the gentle hand,*
>
> *One of that ministering band,*
>
> *Who comes at sickness' stern demand to help us on our way.*
>
> *From sorrow may you ere be free*
>
> *May pains and sickness from you flee*
>
> *And may the ease you brought to me, attend you day by day.*

These were the last words of Allen Raine, who fought her own troubles and sorrow to bring pleasure to millions, by letting them see her vanishing world and read her dreams.

Vaynor, Merthyr Tydfil
Robert Thompson Crawshay, 1879

God Forgive Me

As you drive the short distance out of Merthyr to Vaynor, the scenery changes in an instant. Suddenly you are on twisting country lanes that lead into the rugged hills of the Brecon Beacons. It is so different from what you have left behind, the industrial wasteland that Merthyr became. Even the Crawshays in their grand castle would have recognised this.

It is a journey the Crawshay family would take to this pretty little church every week, for it is not far up the valley, only four miles. A pleasant walk-or ride if it rained- from their grand home in Cyfarthfa to church. Green, isolated, timeless. The air fresh and pure.

You arrive at St Gwynno's church in a place that is completely separated from that world of poverty, suffering, disease. But not death. Of course not. That comes to everyone. We mark it in different ways, that's all. You can see this in any cemetery.

Robert's grave is unmissable. A huge thing surrounded by grand railings. The slab is tinged with encroaching moss. It is monolithic, alien. Thirteen horses dragged it twenty miles from the quarry at Radyr. Eleven tons of granite. Put there, some say, to prevent his soul from rising up at the Resurrection.

No, he was not a popular man.

Robert Thompson Crawshay
Died May 10 1879
Aged 62 Years
God Forgive Me

Enigmatic and troubled

It was never intended that Robert Thompson Crawshay should become an Iron Master. But the death of his brother, drowned whilst crossing the River Severn at Beachley, pushed him into adopting a role for which he was wildly unsuited. He suddenly inherited the family business from his father, the charismatic William Crawshay.

A journey began from success to failure.

Under Robert's leadership the Cyfarthfa iron works entered a long and terminal decline. Already the local iron ore deposits had been exhausted and they began to rely on imports. The business required far more energetic leadership and business acumen than he could provide. His interests and his problems lay elsewhere.

Because you could never really say that he was a happy man.

His family had been at the heart of the unimaginable changes that had transformed Merthyr. It had once been a small village, home to farmers and shepherds. But then came the rapid and uncontrolled expansion, fuelled by the accidents of geology. The iron ore, the coal, the limestone deposits.

Suddenly the town had grown far beyond the capacity of the area to cope. The gentle pastoral life on the edge of the Brecon Beacons disappeared.

To be replaced by a vision of hell.

By 1801 it was the largest town in Wales. Thousands were drawn there by the possibility of regular work. And there was plenty of it. Merthyr was an important place, doing important work. The town provided the materials that defeated Napoleon. But at a considerable cost.

There had never been either adequate water supply or sanitation systems to cope with a population of 40,000. Space was in short supply and houses were crammed closely together, built quickly and cheaply. Water was collected from pumps in the street or from the polluted River Taff. Cholera was rife. In 1849 over 1400 people died of the disease. Infant mortality was high. *Some parts of the town are complete networks of filth, emitting noxious exhalations,'* said a report in 1844.

Whilst the Crawshays and the other ironmasters brought employment and prosperity for some, they were responsible too for squalor and death. Wales, the first industrialised nation on Earth, was built upon foundations of overcrowding and disease and the suffering of the weakest.

At the top of the pyramid, though, were the Crawshays. Their home in Cyfarthfa was an incongruous island of gentility in this poisoned land.

You cannot visit Cyfarthfa Castle as it is now, without being aware of the tremendous contrast that must have once existed. The grand house, the style the chandeliers, the staircases, the panelling. It gives an impression of an ancient family seat. A very short distance away their employees lived in degrading squalor.

The majority of the elegant residence was built by Richard Lugar in only twelve months in 1824. It cost £30,000. It is a house of 365 windows, of gardens and hothouses. It was built to overlook the successful iron works, looking down proudly upon the foundation of their wealth.

Today it is an interesting museum; then it was a symbol of power, a self-contained community that emphasised their prosperity and position. And people died to keep the Crawshays living in such splendour.

Steel began to supersede iron but Robert was unwilling to take up its manufacture. Bessemer Converters were too expensive. He would not invest in the new process, so that his works were left behind. Others took their business. They would never win it back. The success carefully nurtured by his father and grandfather would never return to Cyfarthfa.

Robert's interests lay elsewhere.

In 1846 Robert married Rose Mary Yeates just before her 18th birthday. She was a well-connected and cultured young woman, acquainted with Darwin and Browning. But the marriage did not prosper. He was a complex person and never truly happy. She was ambitious and energetic, with a strong belief in the role and status of women. No compromise. No meeting of minds. They drifted apart and Rose Mary eventually spent most of her time in London.

Initially Robert was not entirely divorced from the community. He began the Merthyr Horticultural Society, he helped establish schools. He particularly enjoyed music and founded the celebrated Cyfarthfa Brass Band. It was founded largely for his own pleasure, so he always ensured that they had the best of everything. But outside of his private and enclosed world, his workers lived in poverty and filth.

Certainly his reputation amongst his workforce swung wildly between hatred and affection. They never knew what to expect of him. Nothing about him was ever straightforward. He rebuilt St Gwynno's Church in Vaynor on condition the parishioners helped towards the costs of rebuilding Cefn Coed church on the northern edge of Merthyr. Why did he do this? Vaynor was his church. He worshipped here. He had huge amounts of money; he could afford to restore it. Yet he had to make some sort of point.

Eventually Robert Crawshay became alienated from his workers. His unwillingness to invest in steel making processes damaged the business and impacted on wages. Threats of strike action and unionisation led to him to close the works for a time in 1875.

He failed at home and at work. An authoritarian figure, inflexible and ultimately lonely, for that very authority was questioned and rejected by those he believed should merely obey. And when they rejected his authority, they rejected him. The plight of the workers and the contrast with their hardships and the comfortable luxury of the Crawshays, provided the perfect conditions for the growth of valley socialism. It was not only the physical landscape that the Crawshays changed. It was also the political landscape.

A stroke in 1860 left Robert Thompson Crawshay profoundly deaf. He replaced music with photography and left a legacy behind of important and historic pictures. He was dedicated to this enthusiasm, investing heavily in new equipment. He had a studio constructed in the castle and a travelling hut that he would take with him to locations in the Brecon Beacons. But his favourite subject of all was his eldest daughter. When his wife retired to London, his life became focused upon Rose Harriette.

He had her pose in exotic costumes, often dressed as a member of the picturesque poor. They were just like rich people, except that they had less money and certainly they lived in fewer rooms than the Crawshays, but they were fragrant and clean. The real poor were just a little way away from Cyfarthfa but dealing with them was more complicated. They were far less attractive and certainly less tractable.

Rose was made to process the films. Robert believed it seems, that his enthusiasm should be hers too. She was less impressed. This is an extract from her diary, 23 March 1868.

Washed a lot of prints, got 3 fresh chilblains; really what with chilblains and chaps from the coldness of the water washing prints and the stains from all the chemicals all over my hands, they are not fit to be seen. It is too bad. I don't believe another lady in the kingdom has such hands.

He possessed her and could not conceive that she could ever desire a life separate from his own. And when he had to confront what the rest of us would regard as right and proper, his response was unpleasant and unreasonable.

In his portraits he looks a stern man. Hard. Inflexible. Certainly thoughtful. Perhaps troubled. He has a heavy beard. There is a distant look in his eyes. Is he a man carrying a burden? A sense of guilt?

Some people would like to think so. They are encouraged by the epitaph he wrote for himself. Finally they say, he showed remorse for the misery his family had inflicted across the generations. "*God Forgive Me.*" Carved upon that enormous eleven-ton granite slab that marks his grave in Vaynor.

Yet it is an enigmatic epitaph.

Forgiveness for what?

See into it what you will. Many have already done so. A final repentance for the sins inflicted upon the working classes? An admittance of his role in creating the hell on earth that was Merthyr?

If only it were so clear-cut.

Rose Harriette had once promised her father that she would never leave him. The promise of a child. But on 23 May 1877 she met a local barrister, Arthur Williams. When she did leave to marry Arthur, her father exacted a spiteful revenge. Her entirely natural desire for a relationship and personal fulfilment, he regarded as a personal betrayal.

He refused to attend her wedding. He added a codicil to his will, disinheriting her children. And we may read remorse into the epitaph, but it isn't necessarily there, for he didn't subsequently change his intentions. He left things exactly as they were in the material world, with no inheritance for his grandsons. He then asked God to forgive him in the afterlife.

Hard and inflexible, like the granite of his tomb.

Whitebrook, Monmouthshire
Violet Pick, 1910

Victor, Violet. Violence

Drive through Tintern and Llandogo, then just before the bridge which crosses the Wye into Gloucestershire, turn left into the maze of narrow country lanes that entwine the Welsh side of the river. Then, in Whitebrook find a dilapidated grave in the precipitous cemetery below the Baptist Chapel, now a holiday rent.

If it was not for the work of the Gwent Family History Society, the identity of the grave and the story that it holds would be lost forever. Even in the short years since their patient cataloguing in 2008, there had been irreversible deterioration. The inscriptions are fading but it is still possible to distinguish the words. John and Amelia Pick are buried with three of their daughters who they lost in a single, terrible year - Gertrude, Hannah and their youngest, twenty-year-old Violet. And poor Violet was murdered by Victor Jones in Monmouth in 1910.

Forgotten in Whitebrook

The murder of Violet Pick created *'intense consternation'* in Monmouth. It has never been the kind of place where such things happen. What seemed to make it worse, was that she was well known in the town as *'a pretty and charming girl.'* But she lay dead on the historic Vauxhall Bridge over the Monnow. She'd been strangled.

An off-duty policeman, Constable Biston, had been alerted by a woman screaming, *'Oh, God! You are killing me!'* at about 10.30 pm and had rushed to the spot with his neighbour Thomas Addis, a flour merchant who brought his lantern. Violet was lying dead in a clump of bushes, whilst Victor Jones, twenty-two years old, was standing by her, mumbling repeatedly, *'Lock me up. I have murdered Miss Pick.'* There was a tightly-pulled white handkerchief round her neck with the ends pushed into her mouth. There was blood on her linen collar, caused when her dental plate with six teeth had shattered. Her hat was found nearby, along with two hat pins bent during the terrible assault. There was no evidence of *'outrage.'* Victor made no attempt to hide his guilt. *'No doubt,'* he said, *'it will be the rope round my neck, and I want it as soon as possible.'*

Violet was a minor celebrity in the town. She was an accomplished singer and was in demand as a soprano in local concerts. She had done well as a pupil at Monmouth High School and had started work as a pupil-teacher at the boys' school in Priory Street. She spent her weekends at home in Whitebrook, but lodged in Agincourt Street during the week. At 8.00 pm on Thursday 3 February 1910, Violet had told another resident that she was going for a walk. According to Victor, they met and wandered around the racecourse. Then they went to the bridge.

The press quickly and simply explained the case. Victor loved Violet, but she discouraged his attentions, since she was engaged to Sergeant Fred Tyler of the King's Own Rifles, who was playing the clarinet as a bandsman in Gosport. However, it wasn't so straight-forward.

In Victor's pocket, the police found a Christmas card from 'Violet L. Pick.' They had recently been seen talking at a dance and Victor's mother gave a reporter a letter Violet had sent him, which was gleefully published. In it, Violet asks him if he has got rid of any of his old girl friends and appears to imply that Fred did not care for her. He hasn't *found it convenient to go out with me again yet, and I very much doubt whether he ever will.'* She ends her letter with 'Love, from your loving Violet *xx galore.'*

Poor Violet was returned to Whitebrook, where it had been confidently anticipated that she would become head mistress of the village school. Her coffin was carried along the winding paths through the village with, appropriately, a wreath of violets and lilies of the valley from Fred Tyler and another from her school. There was also a harp with a broken string from the Monmouth and District Choral Society. When the chapel was reached, two women fainted, and *'several had to be led outside to prevent them creating a scene by their grief.'*

Victor was a fragile personality. He lived with his mother on Dixton Road and had originally worked for the Monmouth Electrical Lighting Works and then for a mineral water manufacturer in Aberdare. A move into a career as an insurance salesman had not gone well and there was some talk that he might like to be an engine driver. Later in court, his mother revealed that her own father had been described as an imbecile and her cousin had died in an asylum. When he was six, Victor fell from the top of a house onto his head and seemed affected ever since. He was depressed and afraid he would do something wrong. He talked about the *'terrible impulses that came to me to do certain things.'* When he saw a motorcar, he wanted to throw himself under it. He had been seeing his own doctor regularly with phantom complaints. He had complained of his heart, kidneys, stomach, and nerves. The doctor warned Victor that if he did not pull himself together, he would end up in an asylum. He certainly regarded Victor as *'feeble minded.'*

Falling in love with Violet, already engaged to a soldier doing manly things like playing the clarinet, was not likely to stabilise his psychic balance. She was a respected member of her community – bright, attractive and talented. She was popular and respected. But how did Victor see himself?

When the case came to court on 15 March 1910, Justice Grantham agreed that Victor was a peculiar boy, but declared he wasn't insane. He could tell the difference between right and wrong. He felt that a well-educated girl like Violet should not have written as she did to Victor, but that the jury should ignore it, as women of that age did not do the same things as they would do later in life. *'It was possible that she was a girl who liked to have two or three strings to her bow.'*

The jury retired and returned a guilty verdict within forty minutes, with a recommendation to mercy because of his age.

There was a bizarre contrast in court when Victor was sentenced. There was the dreadful theatre of Justice Grantham assuming the black cap, saying it was very sad that someone so young would have to suffer the extreme penalty of the law. Victor himself, however, was quite jaunty. He couldn't explain what he had done, merely that God must have called her. *'Thank you, my lord. I shall be in a better land where I shall meet the dear girl,'* he said. He waved to the gallery,' *Ta ta! Goodbye boys. Goodbye all.'*

The Defence appealed against the verdict on procedural issues – the publication of the letter was wrong, there was alleged misdirection of the jury - and also on the grounds of his youth. He could have slipped away into the dark, undiscovered; he could have thrown her into the river. He didn't, so clearly, he must be mad. The appeal failed. The Home Secretary, Winston Churchill, was urged to grant a reprieve and a petition was signed by seven hundred people in Monmouth and in Usk, where he was to die on 29 April 1910. However, a week before the execution, he was visited by *'lunacy experts'* and within days the sentence was commuted to penal servitude for life. He wasn't insane they decided but had *'mental infirmity.'*

He was sent to Parkhurst where he was said to have developed *'a sullen and forbidding-looking countenance.'* He was placed in the section *'set apart for weak-minded inmates'* but found the prison very threatening. *'I was all right at Usk,'* he said, *'but they will do me in down here.'* In 1913 he was transferred to Broadmoor, where he remained for two years and then returned to Parkhurst. Records show that he was released in February 1925 and sent to Chelmsford to work as an engine driver. He seems to have died around 1950, forty years after he had strangled Violet Pick.

And all that time Violet, her life snatched away from her, lay undisturbed, in the soft rain of the Wye Valley.

Where Violet died

And finally…

Cadoxton, Neath
Margaret Williams 1822

The Murder Stone

The Murder Stone, Cadoxton. Never silent

1823
To record
MURDER
The stone was erected
Over the body
Of
MARGARET WILLIAMS
Aged 26
A native of Carmarthenshire
Living in service in this parish
Who was found dead
With marks of violence upon her person
In a ditch on the marsh
Below this chiurchyard on the morning
Of Sunday the 14th of July
!822

Although
The Savage Murderer
Escape for a season the detection of man
Yet God hath set His mark upon him
Either for time or eternity
And
The Cry of Blood
Will assuredly pursue him
To certain and terrible but righteous
Judgment

The Murder Stone is a remarkable thing for a number of reasons. But for me the most striking thing about it are the words and the raw emotions they represent.

It is the anger of it that grabs your attention. It speaks of *murder, violence, savage outcry, blood and judgement.* The words on the stone are the words of Elijah Waring, a local Quaker and well-known orator, who commissioned the stone to express the outrage of the community at the murder of Margaret Williams and their belief in a retribution from which there could never be any escape. The Murderer is truly a man without hope or salvation, for *God hath set his mark upon him.* It reflects too the belief – or indeed the hope – that the murderer won't escape.

It stands out because it is not square to the path. It is at an angle to the others around, positioned to face where everyone was convinced the murderer lived. The stone stretches out an accusing finger with absolute conviction, silently pointing, inflexible, immovable. It was on the main path through the village for all to see. The house at which it is aimed has long since gone, but this permanent accusation has never gone away.

When you see it, you want to find out more – what is this remarkable gravestone about? Why was Margaret Williams murdered?

It is no surprise to learn, of course, that she was pregnant. It had become the great female sin, especially in towns, though things were always little more relaxed in the countryside where it was frequently important to establish fertility before any marriage. But pregnancy was a woman's greatest risk and her greatest crime. And yet you see in her story, and the reaction to it, the essential contradiction of the nineteenth century – an anger that a woman, however fallen, should be murdered and a desperate desire for justice.

Margaret was found dead on Sunday morning, 14 July 1822.

She was an unmarried country girl from Carmarthenshire, from Llangyndeyrn in the Gwendraeth Valley, near Kidwelly. Her father, John Williams was a labourer. She is described as a *fine, healthy young woman,* known for her *industry and cheerfulness.*

Margaret was pregnant, probably at least 16 weeks. And Margaret was adamant about the father of her child. She had announced it confidently on a number of occasions. It was Llewelyn Richard or Richards, the son of the farmer for whom she worked as a servant. He, of course, denied it. There was nothing to prove that he was the father of her child. Paternity, after all, is deniable. Maternity, on the other hand, is a fact, but it is only in recent years has paternity ever been anything other than a matter of opinion. He accused Margaret of being a fantasist, as a country girl on the make. It probably wasn't his child. She was older than Llewelyn and was exploiting his innocence. She could have proved nothing. In May she had moved out of the Richards farmhouse – or had been thrown out – and was now working for *an industrious old man* living in Cadoxton.

On the night before she died, Margaret had been to Neath. 13 July 1822 had been a fine summer's Saturday, though there had been strong wind and ships on their way to Ireland had been forced to take shelter in Milford Harbour. Margaret had gone to buy a sheep's head that was later found in her basket, along with her hat, on the marsh, a short way from her body. She was on her way home. Was it a chance encounter? Was he waiting for her?

She was found lying on her left side in a pill (a stream or ditch) on the salt marsh, in about 30 inches of water with her head submerged. Her body was badly bruised, with marks on her throat and neck and on both arms above the elbow: the marks on her throat *were manifestly caused by strangulation.*

Clearly, he grabbed her, shook her, strangled her, left her in a ditch. And yes, she was pregnant, for they *'opened and examined the body.'*

The newspaper sympathised with the family who were *'summoned to witness the heart-rending and appalling spectacle of their murdered child'*.

Now in these circumstances suspicion, fell immediately upon Llewelyn Richards. But in the days of capital punishment what possible advantage could there be – in this world – to confession? The newspaper always carried reports of recent executions. What incentive was there to confession? So he said nothing.

He was arrested on Tuesday 16 July 1822, and everyone was sure that they had the right man. The newspaper was pleased to announce that he was *'the man generally suspected of having committed the diabolical act.'* But suspicions alone have never been enough.

The problem was that there was no proof. And this was the key point. They couldn't find any evidence. There was nothing to link him to the murder. All Llewelyn had to do was to keep quiet.

We are told that the strongest suspicions existed against the prisoner but that no evidence was adduced to establish his guilt. In fact, the absence of clues was almost proof in itself, for it was merely an example of 'Human wickedness and cunning.' More work was needed. 'The magistrates have declared their resolution to seek out fresh evidence with unremitting scrutiny and it is devoutly to be wished that the inhuman monster who perpetrated this foul and horrid deed may yet be brought to justice.'

So it is not a person they seek. Merely evidence.

The only verdict the jury at the inquest could reach therefore was *'Wilful Murder against some person or persons unknown.'* But everyone knew he had done it. Or thought they knew. We are told that *'The eye of Providence is upon him.'*

Llewelyn may have escaped conviction and execution but what now could he do? His position within his community was untenable. His family will have known this, too.

He fled to Hereford, whilst a donation was sought to build the accusatory headstone. It took a year to have it prepared and erected.

There is a report in the paper on 3 May 1823 about the stone, which had been erected three weeks before and was already a local attraction. People travelled miles to see it; it was the essential destination for a reviving afternoon stroll.

Think about it. The whole community in which your family lives, is absolutely convinced that you carried out a horrible crime. So are complete strangers. They know, in their eyes beyond all reasonable doubt, that you are a murderer. After all, it was so prominently advertised. Perhaps the family had a reputation. Perhaps he had. And they wouldn't let it go.

Eventually, on 16 April 1825, Llewelyn Richards was tried at the Glamorgan Great Sessions in Cardiff for the murder of Margaret Williams in a prosecution brought by her father.

The indictment reads

Accused of murder by beating her and throwing her into a rivulet. The deceased was pregnant and the prisoner suspected of being her father. She used to be a servant of the prisoner's father.

Llewelyn's plea was '*not guilty.*'

But there was still no evidence which could be presented which put him on the marsh on that Saturday night. He was acquitted.

Not long afterwards, he left Swansea on a cargo vessel to start a new life in America or possibly Australia. But his family still had to face that immutable call for vengeance from the graveyard across the road, standing on the main path through the village for all to see, every day. The crime can never quietly slip into the past, whilst those words are set in stone.

Margaret's family sought consolation that, whilst he might escape human justice, there must come an inescapable final reckoning. A greater power is in pursuit. Llewelyn might run- and we can be sure that he did - but he could never hide. And for some, in this anticipation of revenge, there was hope.

The Murder Stone so easily found speaks of tragedy. It speaks of two families scarred. Of two lives taken, a woman and her unborn child. Of lives ruined. It is a crime and pain that endures. There are still flowers placed on Margaret's grave.

This is the local legend, the story that has endured.

However, you won't be surprised to learn that there is a different narrative. It comes from a book by Charles Wilkins of Springfield, Merthyr, published in 1879, fifty years after these events. He says in his Preface that what he tells us is true.

In his version, one of Richards' neighbours called Parry, claimed he had seen Llewelyn and Margaret together on the night of the murder, looking as if they had quarrelled. That is the reason why Llewelyn was arrested but there was no other compelling evidence to suggest that he had actually done it. But in fact, it was Parry who was the killer and he confessed to the crime on his deathbed.

He said he had approached Margaret on the marsh after Richards had gone and, when his advances were rejected, attacked her. His accusation threw the scent off himself, but he couldn't make it stick. But he'd done enough to point the finger, though in all honesty he didn't have to do much. Margaret herself had already prepared the ground in her pregnancy. Everyone had already made their minds up. Parry himself was in the clear.

Did Charles Wilkins really know something? Did the true murderer frame the father of Margaret's unborn child?

Of course, it brings us no closer to the truth. Nothing will now. All we know is that a pregnant woman was murdered, her life, and the potential of her child, snuffed out on a marsh. The passage of time has dissolved an outrage into a curiosity. But the stone is still there, silently pointing, a symbol of divine pursuit.

But I now look at it with some sadness, for it is the stone and the power of Elijah Waring's words that are remembered today, rather than poor Margaret, found dead upon a marsh.

If you have enjoyed this book, and haven't yet read Volume One, which contains thirty similar stories, then you can contact the publishers, Cambria Books at www.cambriabooks.co.uk or the author directly at www.geoffbrookes.co.uk if you would like to buy one.

Both are always happy to hear from interested and interesting readers!

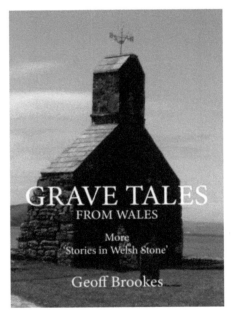

Lightning Source UK Ltd.
Milton Keynes UK
UKHW050300150722
405862UK00006B/238